EXPERIENCING
CHRIST
TOGETHER

Regal

From Gospel Light
Ventura, California, U.S.A.

NEIL T. ANDERSON &
CHARLES MYLANDER

Published by Regal Books
From Gospel Light
Ventura, California, U.S.A.
Printed in the U.S.A.

Regal Books is a ministry of Gospel Light, a Christian publisher dedicated to serving the local church. We believe God's vision for Gospel Light is to provide church leaders with biblical, user-friendly materials that will help them evangelize, disciple and minister to children, youth and families.

It is our prayer that this Regal book will help you discover biblical truth for your own life and help you meet the needs of others. May God richly bless you.

For a free catalog of resources from Regal Books/Gospel Light, please call your Christian supplier or contact us at 1-800-4-GOSPEL *or* www.regalbooks.com.

All Scripture quotations, unless otherwise indicated, are taken from the *Holy Bible, New International Version®*. Copyright © 1973, 1978, 1984 by International Bible Society. Used by permission of Zondervan Publishing House. All rights reserved.

Other versions used are
KJV—King James Version. Authorized King James Version.
*THE MESSAGE—*Scripture taken from *THE MESSAGE.* Copyright © by Eugene H. Peterson, 1993, 1994, 1995. Used by permission of NavPress Publishing Group.
*NASB—*Scripture taken from the *New American Standard Bible,* © 1960, 1962, 1963, 1968, 1971, 1972, 1973, 1975, 1977 by The Lockman Foundation. Used by permission.

Originally published as *The Christ-Centered Marriage* in 1996. Revised and updated version published by Regal Books in 2006.

Library of Congress Cataloging-in-Publication Data
Anderson, Neil T., 1942-
  Experiencing Christ together / Neil T. Anderson, Charles Mylander. — Rev. ed.
    p. cm.
  ISBN 0-8307-4288-3 (hard cover) — ISBN 0-8307-4289-1 (international trade paper)
  1. Spouses—Religious life. 2. Marriage—Religious aspects—Christianity. I. Mylander, Charles. II.
Anderson, Neil T., 1942- Christ-centered marriage. III. Title.
  BV4596.M3A55 2006
  248.8'44—dc22   2006029153

1   2   3   4   5   6   7   8   9   10 · /   10   09   08   07

Rights for publishing this book in other languages are contracted by Gospel Light Worldwide, the international nonprofit ministry of Gospel Light. Gospel Light Worldwide also provides publishing and technical assistance to international publishers dedicated to producing Sunday School and Vacation Bible School curricula and books in the languages of the world. For additional information, visit www.gospellightworldwide.org; write to Gospel Light Worldwide, P.O. Box 3875, Ventura, CA 93006; or send an e-mail to info@gospellightworldwide.org.

CONTENTS

A CULTURAL REVOLUTION

"Boys, get up," Mom called from downstairs.

My brother and I (Neil) didn't want to leave our warm bed. It was cold in the upstairs bedroom loft we shared in that old farmhouse in Minnesota. The floor was like ice, and you could scrape frost off the inside walls in the winter, because the second floor had no heat. We would wait until the last minute (before Dad said something), and then grab our clothes and race downstairs. We dressed in front of the register that poured heat into the first floor from a wood-burning furnace in the basement. Mom always got up at five in the morning to start the fire. Chores had to be done before we ate breakfast. Then we walked our quarter-mile lane to catch the school bus that took us to school in our little country town.

I have great memories of my childhood. Our social life was centered around church, 4-H, school and family gatherings. We didn't have a perfect family—nobody does—but we stayed together. The decade of the '50s was a good time to be raised. Our parents were survivors of the Great Depression and World War II. Patriotism was at an all-time high. The Fourth of July, Memorial Day and Veterans Day were community celebrations. When the National Guard shot off their rifles, a bunch of us boys would race to get the spent cartridges. Families that prayed together stayed together. Only one in a thousand church-going families experienced a divorce.

Then came the '60s. Our country was pulled into a war that many viewed as being simply wrong, and racial segregation could no longer be ignored. Some of our boys went to Canada to avoid the draft. Neighbors moved to the suburbs to avoid busing their children. Our country was being torn apart. Neighbors turned against neighbors, and fathers against sons. Street drugs spread among our college and high school campuses, and the era of "free sex" was ushered in. The Beatles claimed they were more popular than Jesus.

The family was torn apart by this cultural revolution. The debates about war, racism, teenage rebellion, sex, drugs and music polarized the older and younger generations and set parents at odds with their children. Most churches and Christian schools were not preparing leaders for these kinds of conflicts. They offered family-oriented ministries that focused on the "married only once" family in which the father worked and the mother stayed home to raise their children. Today, that model comprises only about 5 percent of the population in an average church.

Family Pressures Changed

It wasn't as difficult to raise good children in the '50s because society basically supported traditional family values. *Father Knows Best, Ozzie and Harriet* and *Leave It to Beaver* were popular television programs. Foul language and explicit sex were forbidden on television and in movie theaters. Children were taught to obey authorities.

Pastoral counseling was taught in seminaries by godly pastors who knew how to pray and apply the Word of God. Few, if any, classes were taught about marriage, because the need for premarital counseling was seldom emphasized. The practical application of ministry focused on preaching, teaching, evangelizing and discipling. Yet seminaries and Bible schools soon began to realize they had to do something to save our families, which were being ripped apart by social changes.

The Catholic church started "Marriage Encounter" to encourage healthy marriages, and the process spread to Protestant denominations.

Evangelical seminaries and Bible schools offered classes on family, marriage and premarital counseling, parenting, and divorce recovery. People debated whether divorce-recovery counseling and single-parenting classes should be offered. Some argued, "Isn't that giving permission to those who are considering divorce by putting a stamp of approval on it?" Others said, "It is our Christian duty to forgive and help these people in need. What's done is done."

Soon, marriage-and-family-related programs, retreats, courses, books and tapes could be found throughout the country. Godly pastors were replaced in pastoral counseling classes by clinical psychologists, all of whom received their doctoral degrees from secular schools, because no Christian schools offered doctoral degrees in psychology in those days. Many of those counselors were (and are) godly people concerned about the family and committed to helping individuals become healthy and functional again. On the other hand, many concerned Christians were troubled by the influence of secular psychology on the Church as well as the demise of evangelism and discipleship.

Today, the most popular radio ministry is Focus on the Family. Gary Smalley's series on marital communication, which was made popular through his infomercials, is one of the best-selling video series of all time—secular or sacred. Books and tapes about marriage and family are consistently the best-sellers, because saving marriages and families is the greatest felt need of our time.

Never in the history of the Church has such a concerted effort been made to save the family. We're thankful for all those who seek to help troubled marriages and families, and we want to acknowledge the incredible contribution these Christian authors and speakers have made. Radio hosts and family advocates are providing important information to the Body of Christ.

However, we need to ask a hard question: How are we doing? Has the family as a whole become stronger in the United States? Have marriages become better? Certainly we can point to the cultural war as a contributing factor, but have we missed something?

The Christian community has searched the Word of God to find the answers for how a husband should love his wife, how a wife should be submissive to her husband, how a mother should mother, how a father should father, and how together they should raise their children. There are many excellent biblical resources available for the following family disciplines that relate to God, society, marriage and parenting:

MARRIAGE AND FAMILY DISCIPLINES

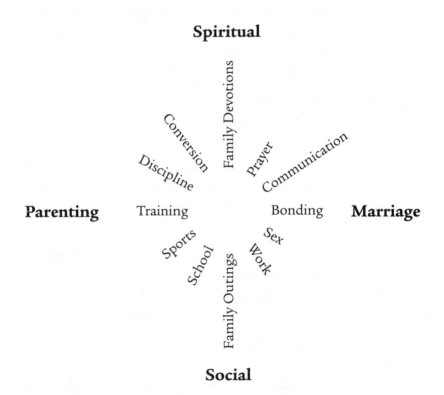

Each discipline is like a spoke in the all-important Christian family wheel. Those in the Christian community learned these disciplines by consulting concordances that directed them to some Old Testament passages and to the second half of Paul's epistles. There, they found biblical instructions for the husband, wife, parents and children. Pastors and teachers preached, taught messages and conducted seminars, workshops and conferences on every one of these spokes in the diagram.

When you read or listen to what committed Christian leaders have to say about these issues, you need to ask yourself, *Are they telling the truth? Are they biblically correct?* In most cases they are. Most Christian leaders try their best to make sure that what they are saying is biblically accurate.

However, something can be right but not complete. We could biblically and accurately communicate what God has to say about parenting, marriage and all the related disciplines, and yet our best efforts to respond may fall short of what God intended. The real question may not be, *What's wrong?* but, *What's missing?*

Just trying to obey biblical instruction often results in a subtle form of Christian behaviorism that sounds like this: "You shouldn't do that. You should do this." Or "Here is a better way to do it." The result will likely be failure as we huff and puff our way into burnout. We may not be legalists in a pharisaic sense, but in too many cases, all we have done is gone from negative legalism (don't do this and don't do that) to positive legalism (do this and do this and do this, ad nauseam). Actually, there is nothing positive about legalism—regardless of its emphasis. When applied to marriage counseling, it sounds like this:

Mr. Jones, you should love your wife as Christ loved the Church. Let me suggest some ways that you could do that. Mrs. Jones, if you would just show your husband a little respect, maybe he would pay more attention to you. The Bible says you should submit to your husband so that the Word of God is not dishonored.

Do you suppose you both could do that for each other? Good! Now let's meet again next week at this same time and see how you are doing.

That may be good advice, and in the right circumstances it can be appropriate, but in many cases it will have little or no lasting effect. Why? Because trying to get people to behave a certain way as a couple without resolving their individual and personal conflicts won't work.

It is not that most Christians don't want to behave appropriately. In many cases, they can't because of unresolved personal and spiritual conflicts. Expecting them to conduct themselves in a healthy way in their marriage relationship would be similar to calling on a star quarterback to play in the Super Bowl when he has the flu and a 103-degree fever. Of course, they would love to play and win the game. None of them has a desire to fail when it comes to such an important life assignment.

Resolving Conflicts

A month after one of Neil's "Living Free in Christ" conferences, a friend called him. She had a friend, who also had attended the conference. Prior to the conference, this lady would call three times a week for prayer. She had other prayer partners whom she called regularly for encouragement and counsel. In addition, she had been seeing a Christian counselor at least once a week. This network of Christian support had been keeping her going.

During the conference, this woman realized that she had been trusting and relying on everyone but God. So she decided not to call any of her friends and not to see her counselor for a month. Instead, she memorized a list of Scripture references showing who she was in Christ and made a commitment to seek first the kingdom of God. A month later, the friend who called Neil said that she could hardly recognize this woman. The woman was a different person because she had resolved her personal and spiritual conflicts and was now living free in Christ.

Please don't misunderstand what we are saying. We all need friends and family to support us, and godly advice has its place. Christian friends and counselors, however, cannot take the place of Christ in our life. Friends can and should encourage us in our faith and help us live a life that is dependent on our heavenly Father.

So, in the previous diagram what we need to add into the process is Christ. The title and the diagram should look like this:

MARRIAGE AND FAMILY
SPIRIT-CONTROLLED DISCIPLINES

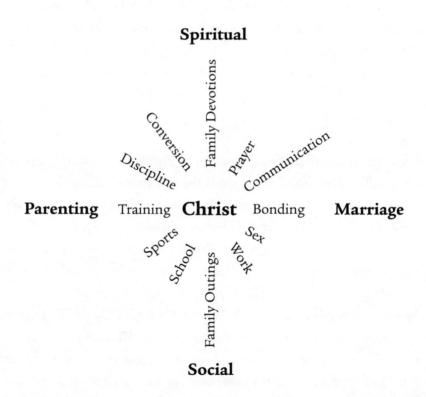

Spiritual

Family Devotions

Conversion

Discipline

Prayer

Communication

Parenting Training **Christ** Bonding **Marriage**

Sports

School

Family Outings

Work

Sex

Social

Maintaining a Christian Marriage

The tendency of the Western Church is to encourage people to live according to the law or godly principles. This is essentially legalism. Under the New Covenant, every born-again Christian is alive in Christ and should live by faith according to what God says is true in the power of the Holy Spirit so that he or she will not carry out the desires of the flesh (see Gal. 5:16-18). A Christian marriage is a spiritual union with God that is intended to be a visible expression of the relationship that God has with the Church, which is the bride of Christ. They are so intertwined that Paul switches from one to the other in Ephesians 5:25-28:

> Husbands, love your wives, just as Christ loved the church and gave himself up for her to make her holy, cleansing her by the washing with water through the word, and to present her to himself as a radiant church, without stain or wrinkle or any other blemish, but holy and blameless. In this same way, husbands ought to love their wives as their own bodies.

We cannot do in the flesh what God by His power can do through us. What makes this difficult to grasp is the fact that all the spokes in the wheel may be biblical and necessary. Indeed, we will add some of our own spokes in this book, but our real purpose will be to connect you and your spouse to the hub of the wheel, which is Christ, so that His life will flow through you. Surely, we want people to behave according to God's standards, but they never will if they are trying to live by godly principles in their own strength. The Law kills, but the Spirit gives life (see 2 Cor. 3:6).

Consider a parallel concept. John 15:8 says, "This is to my Father's glory, that you bear much fruit, showing yourselves to be my disciples." The tendency is to read that passage and conclude that we have to bear fruit. No, we don't! We have to abide in Christ. Bearing fruit is the evidence that we are abiding in Christ. "I am the vine; you are the branches. If a man remains [abides] in me and I in him, he will bear much fruit; apart from me you can do nothing" (John 15:5). We try to bear fruit without abiding in Christ, which is something we simply can't do.

Without Christ we are not just handicapped or limited in what we can do; we cannot do *anything* of eternal significance! We are incomplete without Him, and so are our marriages. To maintain a Christian marriage, we have to become one in Christ. Just saying that won't change anything. It has to be individually appropriated through repentance and faith.

If you will enter into the first half of Paul's epistles, you will do the second half instinctively. This key concept is the presupposition for this book. The behavioral objectives in the second half of the epistles will happen naturally or supernaturally when we abide in Christ. The first set of Paul's epistles establishes us in Christ. If people are established alive and free in Christ, they will grow and their marriages will become healthy. After all, can we truly expect people to behave like Christians when they don't have a clue who they are in Christ? Can we expect husbands to act like Christian husbands when they are not experiencing their freedom in Christ, while trying to serve God in their own strength and resources?

Our advice to struggling couples often sounds like this: *Forget your marriage; you are so torn up on the inside that you probably couldn't get along with your dog right now. But if you are willing to resolve your personal and spiritual conflicts first and get radically right with God, there is great hope for your marriage.*

A Troubled Marriage

A pastor asked Neil if he would counsel a couple on his staff. This was their last resort. If Neil couldn't help them, the couple would likely divorce. They were like two armadillos heading in opposite directions with their tails tied together. Both were defending themselves against the other person's propensity to claw.

Neil told the couple to forget about their marriage. There was no way that any words of advice would change anything for them. Instead, Neil asked the wife if she had a place where she could get away for a couple of weeks. She said she did. So Neil gave her a set of tapes to help her realize who she was in Christ and how she could resolve the bitterness and pain she was experiencing. He encouraged the husband to do the same at home. He asked them not to work through the material for the purpose of saving their marriage, but rather for the purpose of finding their own identity and freedom in Christ. Both the husband and wife said they would.

Neil didn't see or hear from the couple for three years. Then one Sunday after church while he was at a restaurant with his family, he saw the husband with his three children, but no wife. Then, to his surprise, she came in and sat with her husband and children. She had been parking the car. After recognizing Neil, they shared what they had done. Both had found their freedom in Christ, which had made it possible for them to resolve their differences.

The Purpose of This Book

Hundreds of people have spoken to us about their marriages. Many have tried marriage counseling, but with little success. In such cases, we don't continue trying to counsel them as a couple, but instead we help them individually to resolve their personal and spiritual conflicts. The tool we use to accomplish this is called the "Steps to Freedom in Christ."

From experience, we have learned that about 85 percent of couples can work through the individual Steps on their own and that the chances of them gaining freedom in Christ and maintaining it is greatly enhanced if they first read Neil's books *Victory over the Darkness* (Regal Books) and *The Bondage Breaker* (Harvest House). The Steps are included in *The Bondage Breaker*, or they can be purchased separately from Christian bookstores or from the office of Freedom In Christ Ministries (www.ficm.org). The other 15 percent of couples need the help of a trained encourager. That process is explained in Neil's book *Discipleship Counseling* (Regal Books).

We have had the privilege of helping thousands find their freedom in Christ and, in many cases, this has saved their marriage. But we have also discovered that issues still need to be resolved as a couple. That is what this book is all about: setting marriages free in Christ.

We will start with God's perfect design for Adam and Eve and then explain how the Fall and individual sin affects the marriage and family. We will show Christ's plan to restore a fallen humanity and the institution of marriage. We will discuss male and female differences, conflict resolution, communication, finances, sex and, finally, a plan for forgiveness, resolution and restoration.

The last chapter will provide a step-by-step procedure for resolving personal and spiritual conflicts. Many couples work through the process together on their own (as we have done with our wonderful wives), while others study through this material in their churches and then schedule a weekend retreat to facilitate the process. At the end of each chapter are discussion questions to be used in classes. The more intimate and personal questions are reserved for the actual process of going through the "Steps to Setting Your Marriage Free."

If you are planning on using this book as a course in your church, let us encourage you to first go through *Beta, The Next Step in Discipleship* (Gospel Light). This course was designed to enable individuals to become alive and free in Christ. If both husband and wife are alive and free in Christ, then both can easily process this book and the Steps to Setting Your Marriage Free. However, if one spouse cannot or will not deal with his or her own personal issues, establishing oneness in marriage won't be possible. You cannot have corporate freedom without individual freedom. The whole cannot be greater than the sum of its parts.

Note that this is not a theory book. Neil and I have been married many years and are now enjoying our adult children and grandchildren. We are convinced that Christ can resolve the conflicts that keep couples from having good relationships together in Christ. We are not "wonderful counselors"—the Lord Himself is the Wonderful Counselor, and only He can set captives free.

God loves His Church, and marriage was His idea. Yet every married couple will experience difficulty. Some will run from it; others will grow by it. Some will manage their conflicts and coexist; others will learn how to resolve their conflicts and grow together. If you are willing to face the truth and walk in the light, your marriage can be what God wants it to be. The will of God will never lead you where the grace of God cannot enable you to be all that He created you to be. If you are ready to put Christ back into the center of your life and the center of your marriage and home, there is great hope for you. Jesus has an answer, because He is the answer. He is the Bondage Breaker, and He will set your marriage free.

GOD'S PERFECT DESIGN

The LORD God said, "It is not good for the man to be alone. I will make a
helper suitable for him." But for Adam no suitable helper was found.
So the LORD God caused the man to fall into a deep sleep; and while he was
sleeping, he took one of the man's ribs and closed up the place with flesh.
Then the LORD God made a woman from the rib he had taken out of the man,
and he brought her to the man. The man said, "This is now bone of my bones
and flesh of my flesh; she shall be called 'woman', for she was taken out of
man." For this reason a man will leave his father and mother and be
united to his wife, and they will become one flesh. The man and his
wife were both naked, and they felt no shame.

GENESIS 2:18,20-25

Companionship—A Universal Need

If you counted only grades, he was a good student. He came from a missionary family, and he was planning to serve the Lord in the same way he had been taught. He did seem to be a little obsessed with finding the right answer, and he was rather uptight. I (Neil) remember thinking at the time that if I were to tiptoe up behind him and tap him with a little hammer, he would break into a thousand pieces. Yet he was dedicated to the cause of Christ, motivated to do the right thing, and disciplined to accomplish it.

He was also a loner. I never saw him associate with the other students. I passed it off as another example of a missionary kid who had trouble socializing with his own peer group, having been raised in another culture. Too many seminary students, too many people like him, struggle through life without making any lasting friends or personal connections. I always went out of my way to greet him, but our conversations were usually trite and superficial. I had all but forgotten about him when I read in the paper seven years later that the police discovered this frightened young man cowering in a closet of a suburban home after having murdered his parents, whose bodies were found in the living room.

For too many people, life is like riding in those bumper cars at carnivals. "Hi, how are you doing?" Bump! Bump! "Fine, thanks for asking." Bump! Bump! "Good to see you again." Bump! Bump! "Nice day, isn't it?" Bump! Bump! The little cars are our protection to keep others from getting too close to us. We keep bumping into each other superficially, and then one day somebody slips off and in utter despair the unthinkable happens. It is not good for man to be alone.

It is not good for anybody to be alone. A book may be a good companion for a season. We can have a vicarious relationship with our favorite television characters once a week, but they never talk back. A walk in the park is refreshing, but we cannot carry on a two-way conversation with a tree. We can worship creation for a while, but it will not satisfy our need for the Creator. Sitting in a beautiful house alone will be empty loneliness without a companion. Even attending a social function can be a lonely experience if we are disconnected with others in the midst of a crowd. We all have an inner longing for some reciprocal human contact that doesn't violate our fragile existence. Those who think they don't are the ones who are most in need. It is a sad commentary about our existence when we say that a dog is man's best friend!

At times we need to be alone with our thoughts, but sooner or later we need to share with somebody else what we are thinking, seeing, hearing or experiencing. Life was meant to be shared. One of the most basic instincts on seeing a beautiful sunset or hearing some inspiring music is to share it with someone else. We photograph special times and places because we want to share them with someone—anyone. We may look at our old photos for a nostalgic moment alone, but they usually are viewed when friends or relatives visit.

An Eternal Need

It seemed as though Adam had it all. God formed him out of the dust of the ground and then breathed into him the breath of life. Adam was physically alive. His ability to feel, think and experience the environment around him was synchronized with his physical body. He was a living, breathing, walking and talking man created in the image of God.

His soul lived in harmony with his body. More important, he was also spiritually alive. His soul was in perfect union with God.

Adam knew who he was and why he had been created. His purpose and responsibility was to rule the rest of God's creation. God placed him in the "Garden of Eden to work it and take care of it" (Gen. 2:15). Further, Adam was afforded a tremendous amount of freedom as long as he remained in a dependent relationship with his Creator. Adam seemed to have a perfect life and could have lived forever in the presence of God. He was unconditionally loved and accepted by his heavenly Father and had no concept of insecurity. All his deepest needs of life—identity, acceptance, security and significance—were met in creation and sustained by the presence of his heavenly Father. Yet Adam was lacking something: a relationship with a peer. He needed someone like himself with whom to share all the good things God had created.

Our relationship with God is not based on equality; it is based on His sovereignty and our necessity. Without Him, we don't exist. He is the Creator; we are the creation. He is the Infinite; we are the finite. He is the Potter; we are the clay. Yet we are unique in all of creation. God spoke and the heavens were formed, but God did not speak man into existence. He took dust and breathed His own life into him (see Gen. 2:7). This synthesis of divine breath and earthly dust is what sets us apart from the animal kingdom and describes our basic nature.

The unique purpose and position of humanity may be why God paraded all the animals in front of Adam and had him name them. No animal could fulfill Adam's need to belong. It wasn't that the giraffe was too tall, the elephant too big or the monkey too silly. It was that Adam needed someone who was his equal in creation—someone who was spiritually alive and created in the image of God. He needed someone like himself.

God could reason and communicate with His own trinitarian self. Notice the inner communication within the Godhead in the creation account: "Then God said, 'Let *us* make man in *our* image, in *our* likeness'" (Gen. 1:26, emphasis added). Although this represents the Hebrew plural of majesty, it also suggests communion among Father, Son and Holy Spirit. Further, the animals could interact with each other, but Adam was alone. Adam could not be mentally, emotionally and spiritually compatible with someone who wasn't of his own kind. So God created a suitable helpmate for him.

Like Adam, the woman was not spoken into existence with the rest of creation. Unlike Adam, however, she was not an independent creature taken from the dust. She was related to man in creation. God formed the woman from a part of the man. Adam knew the difference instantly and proclaimed, "This is now bone of my bones and flesh of my flesh; she shall be called 'woman,' for she was taken out of man" (Gen. 2:23). The woman was not created to have a status independent from man, and man was no longer independent from her. They were not created to be in competition with each other. Eve came into being by the power of God, from man, for whom she is called to be a helpmate. She is the only suitable helper for him.

Adam was drawn to Eve the moment he saw her. They saw each other as male and female, yet one flesh. They recognized both their differences and their oneness. God used their masculinity and femininity to both differentiate them and unite them. They were naked and unashamed. Sexual attraction and passion were present before the Fall. Sex was not evil; it was God's plan. The Fall perverted what God had created to be good.

A Covenant Relationship

The Lord bestows favor and honor on those people whose walk is blameless (see Ps. 84:11). The man is honored by the acknowledgment that the woman was created for him. The woman is honored by the acknowledgment that the man is incomplete without her. In humility, the woman acknowledges that she was made for man. In humility, the man acknowledges that he is incomplete without the woman. Both share an equal dignity, honor and worth because of their created purpose. Both share a common humility and honor before God and each other. Each is necessary for the completion of the other. Both absolutely need God, and both necessarily need each other. They were created to live in an interdependent relationship with each other and a mutually dependent relationship with God.

Relationships are the heart of life, and the relationship between the male and the female is the earthly expression of the relationship between God and humankind. Interestingly, the first comment in Scripture about the creation of Adam and Eve relates to sexuality: "Male and female he created them" (Gen. 1:27). Thus, even our sexuality relates us to the image of God. Because adultery and fornication are forbidden, marriage represents the essence of life, which is relationship. It has its source in the eternal fellowship of the triune God: Father, Son and Holy Spirit.

Although many close and wonderful relationships are described in Scripture, such as that between Jonathan and David, we can experience only two covenant relationships in this life. Both are based on God's Word and rooted in His character. The first and foremost is our covenant relationship with God. The second is the marriage between a man and a woman. This covenant relationship may include children until they are grown and leave the home. All other meaningful relationships are contractual or mutually convenient. Although two people can have a covenant relationship with God—and consequently have fellowship or spiritual kinship one with the other—they don't have a covenant relationship with each other unless they are married to each other.

Contracts are usually drafted to protect all parties involved in case any one of the parties defaults or fails to fulfill his or her side of the bargain. They can be written contracts, which are legally binding, or verbal agreements, which are sealed with a handshake. In either case, the innocent parties can seek legal action for a breach of contract or simply be no longer obligated to fulfill their sides of the agreement should the others not fulfill theirs. Contracts ensure that all involved fulfill their word and provide an escape clause should the contract be broken.

Covenants are promises for one person to fulfill his or her word irrespective of the other person. Covenants are made to last regardless of the circumstances. While contracts provide for natural disasters or human failures that are beyond the right or ability of either party to control, covenants don't make such provisions. Honoring covenants is not dependent on things we have neither the right nor the ability to control. We are eternally grateful that the covenant relationship we have with God is not based on whether we can perfectly keep our end of the bargain. He will keep His Word whether we do or not.

Wedding vows are a covenant commitment that we make to stay faithful as a husband or wife, for better or for worse, for richer or for poorer, in sickness and in health, until death separates us. When we were married, we made a covenant commitment to our spouse, which we intended to keep whether our spouse did or not. Our spouse did the same. Nothing and no one on planet Earth—other than ourselves—can keep us from being the husbands and wives God created us to be.

At some point in Church history, the tradition of exchanging rings was inaugurated. Rings were a visible sign that sealed the covenant. They were to be publicly worn so that others could see the couple had become one in Christ and were "off the market." The rings also served as a reminder to the couple of the vows they had made publicly.

A covenant relationship is unique from all others not just because it is based on love, but also because it is a lifelong commitment. We are commanded to love all humankind. What makes marriage unique is commitment. What makes marriage great is love and romance.

Author Michael P. Horban says the following about this amazing covenant relationship:

Marriage License—A Learner's Permit

It's a wise groom who has to be dragged to the altar. He knows what love is. It's death! If the lovers don't know this, they're headed for trouble. Never will you have your way again. You can't be happy if the other person isn't. No matter who wins the argument, you lose. Always. The sooner you learn this, the better off you'll be.

Love is an exercise in frustration. You leave the window up when you want it down. You watch someone else's favorite television program. You kiss when you have a headache. You turn the music down when you like it loud. You learn to be patient without sighing or sulking.

Love is doing things for the other person. In marriage two become one. But the one isn't you. It's the other person. You love this person more than you love yourself. This means that you love this person as he or she is. We should ask ourselves frankly what that impulse is that makes us want to redesign the other person. It isn't love. We want the other person to be normal, like us! But is that loving the other person or ourselves?

Love brings out the best in people. They can be themselves without artificiality. People who know they're loved glow with beauty and charm. Let this person talk. Create the assurance that any idea, any suggestion, any feeling can be expressed and will be respected. Allow the other person to star once in a while. A wife's joke doesn't have to be topped. Don't correct your husband in the middle of his story. Cultivate kind ways of speaking. It can be as simple as asking them instead of telling them what to do.

Don't take yourself too seriously. Married life is full of crazy mirrors to see ourselves—how stubborn, how immature we really are. You may be waiting for your wife to finish because you never lifted a finger to help her.

Love is funny. Its growth doesn't depend on what someone does for you. It's in proportion to what you do for him or her. The country is swarming with people who have never learned this. So are divorce courts.[1]

All relationships other than marriage are intended for mutual convenience, such as those we share with friends, roommates, coworkers and neighbors. These relationships are important and, in many ways, necessary for life, as no one is an island. However, they are not covenant relationships. Many disappointments come when we begin to live as if they were and develop expectations of others that we have no right to assume. Some people can be deeply hurt when a roommate moves out or a friend starts to drift away because of other interests. Engagements can be broken, but marriage is supposed to be for life once the vows have been said.

Children are born to leave. The psalmist said, "Your wife will be like a fruitful vine within your house; your sons will be like olive shoots around your table. Thus is the man blessed who fears the LORD" (Ps. 128:3-4). There is a major difference between a vine and an olive shoot. A vine is connected to some other form of life and cannot operate independently of it. An olive shoot is not; it is similar to a potted plant. It was created separately and intended to be transplanted some day. In the same way, the child in the womb is not a part of the mother's body, although the baby is carried and nurtured by the mother. Children grow up and leave their mother and father, while maintaining close ties to their family. Most will seek their own covenant relationship in marriage and bear their own children.

Convenience relationships are similar to two pieces of paper that are held together with a paper clip. With care, they can be easily separated and will leave little imprint on each other. In attempting to tear them apart without removing the paper clip, however, some damage will occur.

With contractual relationships, the two pieces are stapled together. Both pieces are free to do their own thing, except in the place they are stapled together. Damage is done when one is torn from the other, although the individual content of each page is left intact.

In covenant relationships, the pages are glued, or bonded, together. The two have become one. Lasting damage will be done to both if they are separated. "For this reason a man will leave his father and mother and be united to his wife, and they will become one flesh. The man and his wife were both naked, and they felt no shame" (Gen. 2:24-25).

Criteria for a Successful Marriage

Most conservative scholars credit Moses for writing the first five books of the Old Testament. In the above passage from Genesis 2:24-25, Moses both narrates and instructs: Adam and Eve did not have parents to leave, but they were naked and unashamed. Marriages would be a lot easier if neither spouse had any ancestral baggage to bring into the marriage—and it would be a piece of cake if neither had sinned.

The following points reveal three essential criteria for a successful marriage:

1. First, both the husband and wife need to leave Mom and Dad—physically, emotionally, mentally, spiritually and financially. However, they are still commanded to honor their parents.

2. Second, they need to bond together in such a way that they become one.

3. Third, they need to have no unresolved issues between themselves and God so that intimacy and transparency are the norm for their relationship.

Let's briefly look at these three criteria, which will be further explained throughout the remainder of this book.

Leaving Mom and Dad

It does not take long for newly married couples to realize they did not marry a single person with no ancestral heritage. In fact, they usually become painfully aware of this during the engagement period. Some probably wonder, *Can't I just have this wonderful person without the family and all their problems? I can handle the parents, but do I have to accept that brother and weird uncle?*

Since Adam and Eve, nobody marries a new creation without ancestral or cultural baggage. We marry into three or four generations of family heritage, including all the accompanying customs, habits and patterns of doing things. Some family traditions can be healthy, others are destructive. The cycles of abuse that pass from one generation to another are well-attested social phenomena of our times.

It is important for us to consider in what ways we have not left our mom and dad and what patterns of behavior we have brought into our marriage that are not conducive to a stable relationship. Separating from parents and setting aside destructive behavior patterns comprise the first two issues that need to be resolved in setting a marriage free. We cannot change our family heritage or fix the past, but we can all be free from the past by the grace of God.

Of course, we need to keep in mind that this is not a license to dishonor our parents or an admonition to cut off family ties. Listen to the interchange between Jesus as an adult and His mother, Mary, in a public setting:

On the third day there was a wedding in Cana of Galilee, and the mother of Jesus was there; and Jesus also was invited, and His disciples, to the wedding. And when the wine gave out, the mother of Jesus said to Him, "They have no wine." And Jesus said to her, "Woman, what do I have to do with you? My hour has not yet come." His mother said to the servants, "Whatever He says to you, do it" (John 2:1-5, *NASB*).

Jesus was not being impertinent. "Woman" was a term of respectful address, but He was also saying to His mother that He was no longer subject to her, but rather to His heavenly Father. She immediately stepped back and told the servants to obey Jesus. Yet if we think for a moment that Jesus no longer respected or cared for His mother, we need to listen to His words on the Cross:

When Jesus saw his mother there, and the disciple whom he loved standing nearby, he said to his mother, "Dear woman, here is your son," and to the disciple, "Here is your mother." From that time on, this disciple took her into his home (John 19:26-27).

What a wonderful model! Jesus showed respect and concern for His mother and even provided for her after His departure by asking John to look after her. Our role as parents is not to raise good little children who will do our bidding as long as we can control them. It is our calling to raise responsible adults who will learn to do the will of God. Remember, they are potted plants, not clinging vines.

We have talked to many older adults who are still trying to earn the approval of their parents. Many young adults are still financially dependent on their parents. Some parents even use money as a way of controlling their adult children. Neil counseled a middle-aged lady who made decisions about her home and family based on whether she thought her mother would approve. The mother was dangling a sizable estate over her head. This same mother had already disinherited one of her children whom she could not control or manipulate.

We are usurping God's place in our adult children's lives when we try to control and manipulate them with conditional love and acceptance, threaten them with disinheritance, or insist they honor us. Parents need to repent of such attempts at controlling their children, and their children need to renounce ever putting faith in these sinful influences on their lives. Consider the following questions:

- Does the approval of relatives (or any other mortal) mean more to you than the approval of God?
- Are you still trying to live up to the expectations of your parents or siblings?
- Is your relationship with God the most important relationship in your life?
- Is your relationship with your spouse the second most important relationship in your life?
- Would you be willing to sever any other relationship that would threaten your relationship with God or your spouse, even if it meant cutting yourself off from members of your immediate family?
- In what ways have you not left your mother and father: Physically? Spiritually? Mentally? Emotionally? Financially?

Neil once met a young wife and mother of two children who wept openly as she considered the need to forgive her mother. "I can choose to forgive her now," she said, "but what do I do this Sunday when I go over to her house and she verbally abuses me all over again?" He encouraged her to put a stop to that way of thinking. "But aren't I supposed to honor my mother?" she asked.

How would it honor this woman's mother to allow her to systematically destroy the daughter's present marriage and family with her verbal abuse? If the daughter does not free herself from such abuse and set scriptural boundaries to protect herself and her family from further damage, she will likely do the same to her children and grandchildren. In the Old Testament, the primary thrust of honoring one's mother and father was to financially look after them in their old age, usually by moving them into the eldest son's home (see Exod. 20:12; Deut. 5:16).

As parents, we are to love our adult children and support them in all that God leads them to do, but we have relinquished all control of them. They are no longer our children to raise. We gave them away. They are adult children of God. We want them to have self-control, which comes from abiding in Christ. By the grace of God, we will lend physical, spiritual, mental, emotional and financial support to our children when it is appropriate or possible.

Our prayers should be that we would never do anything that would supplant God's place in their lives. Our children will honor us most by becoming the people God wants them to be. We have done the best we could to raise children who would leave us and cleave to someone else. We have given away our "potted plants." Someday, they will do the same. We were not perfect parents, and our children will undoubtedly have to renounce less than perfect habits they picked up from us.

The Bible does not elaborate on what it means to leave a mother and father. Certainly, some circumstances make complete separation difficult: Physically leaving a mother and father in nomadic tribes may be inadvisable for the sake of survival and safety, and financial separation may not be possible when it comes to family-owned businesses. However, whatever the circumstances, in order to protect the covenant relationship of marriage, contractual agreements (written or verbal) should be made to ensure that the newly married couple has their own space and financial freedom. The Holy Spirit will convict one or both spouses when there is an unholy attachment to a parent that keeps the couple from having a oneness in Christ.

Becoming One

The second essential ingredient for a successful marriage is oneness. Bonding is not a given. You can have a house full of Christians and not have a Christian home. Two people can live together and be legally married according to the government, but they are just two people living together. Somehow, the Lord intends that the two become one. Jesus commented on this important issue in Mark 10:7-9:

> For this reason a man will leave his father and mother and be united to his wife, and the two will become one flesh. So they are no longer two, but one. Therefore what God has joined together, let man not separate.

This mystical union between a man and a woman is both spiritual and physical. Adam and Eve were to be fruitful and multiply (see Gen. 1:28). Becoming one flesh certainly includes sexual union, which may result in the conception of a child. The two become one in procreation.

Sexual union can also be abused. Paul teaches that a man can join himself to a harlot and become one flesh (see 1 Cor. 6:16). The two are not married, however, in the eyes of God. Jesus said, "What *God* has joined together, let man not separate" (Matt. 19:6, emphasis added). Adam and Eve were spiritually alive. Their souls were in union with God. In marriage, they were joined by God.

Most Christian ministries understand the threefold process of marriage as leaving, cleaving and becoming one flesh. What some fail to acknowledge is that marriage must also be in accordance with the laws of the land, because all authority has been established by God. It includes a public declaration by the couple, in front of witnesses, that they will take each other as husband and wife. Then they exchange vows, which establish the marriage as a covenant relationship. Finally, they consummate their marriage by becoming one flesh. The glue that holds the two together is the relationship that each spouse has with God. The strongest architectural design is an equilateral triangle (i.e., all three sides are equal):

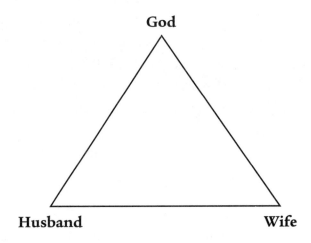

Should either side of the triangle be broken or weakened, it will dramatically affect the strength of the marriage. That is why Paul states we are not to be unequally yoked:

> Do not be yoked together with unbelievers. For what do righteousness and wickedness have in common? Or what fellowship can light have with darkness? What harmony is there between Christ and Belial? What does a believer have in common with an unbeliever? (2 Cor. 6:14-15).

Bonding takes place between a man and a woman when there is a total commitment of body, soul and spirit to each other, without reservation. Adam and Eve bonded in the presence of God. Together they were naked and unashamed. Nothing about their bodies was "dirty," and a sexual relationship between a husband and a wife was not separate from an intimate relationship with their Creator. They had not sinned and there was nothing to hide; therefore, there was no reason to cover up. They were naked and unashamed! That was God's perfect creation and design for marriage. Such was the case for Adam and Eve, but such is not our case.

Developing Intimacy

The Fall of humankind clipped two sides of the triangle. Sin separated us from God. The man and woman were left alone to relate to one another without God. Now, only in Christ can we be restored. Only then can our marriages become what God intended them to be.

Before we look at the consequences of the Fall and what must happen for our marriages to be free in Christ, we need to ask ourselves a question: *Would we be willing to work toward intimacy and transparency before God and our spouse?* We are called to walk in the light (see 1 John 1:7) and to speak the truth in love (see Eph. 4:15). If that is not happening between us and our spouse, there is little chance of experiencing the oneness we have in Christ.

In Conclusion

An old godly pastor referred to a time when he was newly married. He had sown some wild oats and done other things of which he was ashamed. He had never told his wife, and he was ashamed to tell her now. He didn't want anything to come between them, though, and he always feared she would find out about some of his escapades from another source. So one day, he wrote down all the things he had done.

He lacked the courage to just confess it to his wife face to face. So he asked her to sit and listen while he read all that he had written.

Without looking up, he asked her what she thought.

"Charlie," she said, "there isn't anything you could share with me that, just by having you share it, wouldn't cause me to love you more."

That is love in action. Will you be that kind of spouse—one who is willing to share, forgive and accept the other person, warts and all? If that is your heart's desire, close this chapter with the following prayer:

Dear heavenly Father, I acknowledge You as the Lord of my life. Thank You for my own salvation. I deserved eternal damnation, but You gave me eternal life. I want to be merciful as You have been merciful to me and to forgive as You have forgiven me. Now I ask You to give me the grace to accept my spouse in the same way that You have accepted me. Give me the courage to speak the truth and the grace to do it in love. I desire to have an intimate and transparent relationship with You and my spouse. I commit myself to be the husband/wife that You created me to be. I desire our marriage to be one in Christ, an indissoluble union in which we are free from our pasts. Lead us into the truth that will set us free in Christ. In Jesus' precious name I pray.

Note

1. " 'Men Are from Mars . . .' Part 3—Ephesians 5:23-24," *Countdown!* Golden Minutes Ministries Newsletter, October 1996, cited at "Sermon Illustrations," *Bible.org*. http://www.bible.org/illus.asp?topic_id=913 (accessed July 2006).

Group Discussion

1. Why should a Christian marriage be understood as a covenant relationship as opposed to a contractual or convenience relationship?

2. What are the potential negative consequences for marriages if spouses do not leave their mother and father and cleave only to God and one another?

3. How can a couple become one? Can this happen physically but not spiritually?

4. What happens to a marriage when one spouse is one with God and the other isn't?

5. What are the barriers to an intimate relationship?

Devotional Guide for Couples

Read Matthew 19:3-6 and discuss what God originally intended for marriages.

NURTURE AND NATURE

Wives, in the same way be submissive to your husbands so that, if any of them do not believe the word, they may be won over without words by the behavior of their wives, when they see the purity and reverence of your lives. Your beauty should not come from outward adornment, such as braided hair and the wearing of gold jewelry and fine clothes. Instead, it should be that of your inner self, the unfading beauty of a gentle and quiet spirit, which is of great worth in God's sight.

Husbands, in the same way be considerate as you live with your wives, and treat them with respect as the weaker partner and as heirs with you of the gracious gift of life, so that nothing will hinder your prayers. Finally, all of you, live in harmony with one another; be sympathetic, love as brothers, be compassionate and humble. Do not repay evil for evil or insult with insult, but with blessing, because to this you were called so that you may inherit a blessing.

1 PETER 3:1-4,7-9

Perhaps you have heard or said the following:

- If you want to see what your fiancée will look like in 20 years, just look at her mother.
- Like father, like son.
- He's a chip off the old block.
- What can you expect from him, given who his parents are?
- He's the spittin' image of his old man.

"Spittin' image" is a slang conjunction of "spirit and image." In other words, one has the same spirit and image as that of his or her parent. Is there any truth to those clichés? Are we destined to be like our parents?

Heredity or Environment?

Not me! you may be thinking. *No way am I going to be like my old man.* Yet even in this, the "old man" is still influencing who you are or are not going to be: The guiding principle influencing your behavior and choices is *to be or not be like another person.* Such thinking has set many up for failure. In a truly Christian marriage, both spouses should be in the process of becoming like Christ, not trying to be or not be like some other mortal.

To what degree are we products of our past? Are we just biological offspring of our parents? Have our personalities and habits been totally shaped by our upbringing? Educators have asked these questions for centuries. The secular debate is usually about the prominence played by the environment as opposed to genetics. Is it nurture or is it nature that most influences who we will become? It is generally accepted that genes and hormones prescribe physical features and predispose us to certain physical strengths and weaknesses.

On the other hand, nobody questions that the homes in which we were raised, the schools we attended and the communities in which we played all affected how we think and the way we developed. Chances are we will discipline our children in the same ways we were disciplined and relate to our spouses in the same ways our mothers and fathers related to each other. They were the only models we had during our early development. Unless we make concentrated efforts to reprogram our minds and retrain our habits, we will bring into our marriages all that we have been taught in the past.

Our struggles, however, are not only confined to the less-than-perfect atmosphere in which we were raised and the fleshly lusts of our fallen natures. We also have to contend with the god of this world. Scripture teaches that there are inherited spiritual bents toward certain sins. From the Ten Commandments, we learn that iniquities are passed on from one generation to the next. In the New Testament, Peter refers to our "futile way of life inherited from [our] forefathers" (1 Pet. 1:18, *NASB*).

For instance, Abraham lied about his wife to save his own neck. He told the Egyptians that she was his sister (see Gen. 12:10-20). His son Isaac did exactly the same thing (see 26:7). Isaac's son Jacob lied about everything, and 10 of his sons lied about selling his favorite son, Joseph, into slavery. Joseph, however, was given three major opportunities to save himself by lying, but he would not.

How do we explain all this? Coincidence? Modeling? It is doubtful that it was just the latter, because Isaac hadn't yet been born when his father lied. So Did Abraham teach Isaac to lie about his wife? We seriously doubt that Abraham said to Isaac, "Listen, son, if your life is ever threatened because others lust after your wife, just tell them she is your sister. I tried it once. It turned out to be a bad decision, but maybe it will work for you."

Consider a more modern example. A well-known pastor committed adultery. It was a devastating experience for him, his church, his marriage, his family and the thousands who had looked to him as their spiritual leader. Not too many knew, however, that this man's father was a pastor who had committed adultery and left the ministry. His older brother also was a pastor who had committed adultery and left the ministry. How do we explain that? Bad genes? Chances are, this gifted pastor said at one time, "That is never going to happen to me!" But it did.

In what ways are we products of our pasts, and how have the sins of our ancestors affected us and our marriages? In addition to considering what we inherited, we need to also understand the subtle differences between the human nature of men and women. Concerning ourselves with these issues is necessary if we believe that Christ is the answer and desire to have a Christ-centered marriage. (For additional study on the importance of ancestral bloodlines, how iniquities are passed on from one generation to another, and what to do about them, see *Discipleship Counseling* [Regal Books].)

Differences Can Be Strengths

Let's first consider how we should understand the differences in basic human nature between men and women. Are such natural differences a potential pitfall for marriages, or did God design us as complementary pairs in order to further our sanctification? We believe God intended our differences to be the strength of our marriages, as long as they are complementary and not competitive.

When I (Neil) taught a Sunday School class for young married couples, I often used a teaching technique that required the class to either agree or disagree with several statements. I would have them gather in *agree* or *disagree* groups to find biblical support for their positions, allowing them time to prepare for sharing their insights and perspectives with the others.

Two men from the class took me out for lunch one day. They were good Christian friends, but they were having a problem with my teaching technique.

"What's your concern?" I asked.

"We don't believe you should use the 'agree or disagree' statements in Sunday School."

"Why is that?"

"Well, sometimes our wives don't agree with us!"

I really don't know how I kept a straight face! I can't even restrain myself from laughing as I write this.

These two men remind me of the old farmer when he first got married. He had always been taught that the husband was supposed to be the head of the home. As such, he had to make sure the right perspective was brought to bear on all issues, which, of course, was his own perspective. Then the farmer grew up a little and began to tolerate his wife's perspective. Then he grew up a little bit more and began to appreciate his wife's perspective. Then he grew up a little bit more and began to seek his wife's perspective. Her perspective was just as valid as his, albeit quite different. Being an intelligent man, he finally figured it out: His wife was a helpmate, not a farmhand.

Differences imply conflict. However, marriages can potentially thrive on conflict in a constructive sense. No husband and wife will see life from the same perspective, nor perfectly agree about how life should be lived. Let me illustrate this point with an example from my own life. When our son was only two years old, he fell and scratched his knee. Given the way my father raised me, I was inclined to say, "Get up, son, and be a man." Joanne was more likely to say, "Oh! Poor baby." Now, after 40 years of marriage, I respond to my grandchild when he falls by saying, "Get up, poor baby!" Then I hug him, throw him up in the air and tickle him until he starts to laugh. Joanne now says, "Poor baby, get up!" Then she holds him until he stops crying. We have had that kind of effect on each other. Little boys need both their mothers and their fathers, and we need each other.

I was raised on the farm in Minnesota; Joanne was raised in the city in Minneapolis. I was an outgoing kind of person; Joanne liked to read and study. I liked contemporary music; Joanne liked classical music. I liked the outdoors; Joanne liked the indoors. I liked roast beef, mashed potatoes and gravy; Joanne liked gourmet food. I came from an intellectually competitive family; Joanne watched in horror as we "played" family games. I came from a family of five; she is an only child. God couldn't have picked a better helpmate. We are like a hunk of red and green clay, all rolled together in one ball. Traces of both the red and the green are visible, but the overall appearance is a combination of both.

We had one other major difference when we were first married. I enjoyed getting up early in the morning. I like to sing in the shower. That was the best I was going to feel all day, and I wanted to tell the world about it. Joanne was a night person. One day, she approached me with Bible in hand and said, "Babe, I have a verse for you." Then she read Proverbs 27:14: "If a man loudly blesses his neighbor early in the morning, it will be taken as a curse."

"Let me see that," I said. Sure enough, that's what it said! I was speechless, until I saw the next verses: "A quarrelsome wife is like a constant dripping on a rainy day; restraining her is like restraining the wind or grasping oil with the hand" (vv. 15-16).

"Look, Joanne," I said. "There is your verse!" Isn't God great?

Surrendering the Advantage

Have you ever tried to restrain the wind or grasp oil with your hand? You can't. So what does this passage in Proverbs 27:15-16 mean? It doesn't make much sense unless you understand that wind and oil represent the Spirit. It is my contention that a natural man cannot contend with a woman's spirit.

What do most men do when they know they can't win? They don't play the game. They lose themselves in their careers, sit in front of their television sets, play sports or work on their hobbies in the garage. Consequently, the functional head in most homes is the wife. Men, however, are physically stronger. Throughout most of recorded history, it was the men who ruled by brute force. They fought the wars, plowed the fields, and shot the game. In many cultures today, women are subjected to demeaning roles because of male physical dominance.

Christianity elevates the status of women wherever the gospel is shared. Men are taught not to use their physical advantage to dominate but to provide and protect. Men are told not to manhandle their wives—physically abusing them is totally against Christian principles. So, if men voluntarily surrender their physical advantage, what happens when women don't do the same with their spiritual advantage? The question will no longer be, Who rules the roost? It will be, Who rules the rooster? What should women do? According to 1 Peter 3:1-4, they should voluntarily choose to be submissive and adopt a quiet and gentle spirit, which has great worth in God's sight. In turn, men should not dominate physically but should strive to be strong in God's Spirit.

After I shared that truth from 1 Peter at a church conference, a young lady said, "Now I understand what happened last night." She explained how she had been nagging her husband while they were driving to a function. She wouldn't stop, no matter what he did. Finally, he got so angry that he pulled the car over, got out and walked home. He just left her sitting there and retreated to his cave. In his mind, what he did was probably better than the alternative.

Being in a submissive role is like riding in the passenger seat of a car. Nobody has a problem riding shotgun, provided two things are true about the driver. First, the driver needs to know where he is going, or at least be willing to ask for directions. If I as a passenger know where we should be going and the driver doesn't, my natural instinct is to say, "Slide over, buster, and let me drive or let me out." Second, the driver needs to obey the rules of the road. When the driver is running red lights, going the wrong way down one-way streets and turning corners on two wheels, the survival instinct of any rider is to get out of the car or say, "Slide over, buster, and let me drive!"

The Responsibility of Leadership

So why do Christian women find it so difficult to be submissive? The primary reason may not be women's liberation; it may be the lack of male spiritual leadership. To be submissive to a leader who seems unable or unwilling to lead creates a great deal of anxiety for anyone, male or female. Many men would bolt or rebel under the same circumstances in which women often find themselves. Being the head of the home is not a right to be demanded; it is an awesome responsibility. Husbands will have to stand before God one day and give an account for what has been entrusted to them.

In the New Testament, when the sons of Zebedee were striving for positions of honor with Jesus, the Lord used the opportunity to teach a critical lesson about leadership. He said we should not be like the rulers of the Gentiles, who lord it over others. "Instead, whoever wants to become great among you must be your servant, and whoever wants to be first must be your slave—just as the Son of Man did not come to be served, but to serve, and to give his life as a ransom for many" (Matt. 20:26-28). Nobody is lower in position than a servant or a slave. So how does this teaching apply to being the head of the home? By describing the nature of the husband's responsibility. Every husband, as the provider and protector, is subject to the needs of his wife and children.

Yet a husband simply cannot meet all of his wife's needs. Only Christ can meet every essential need. That is why every husband should be the spiritual leader, taking whatever steps are necessary to ensure that Christ is the center of his life, his marriage and his family. The best way to ensure that his wife and children become all that God wants them to be is by being all that God wants him to be as a husband and a father.

Paul lays it on the line concerning what we must teach regarding these matters:

> You must teach what is in accord with sound doctrine. Teach the older men to be temperate, worthy of respect, self-controlled, and sound in faith, in love and in endurance. Likewise, teach the older women to be reverent in the way they live, not to be slanderers or addicted to much wine, but to teach what is good. Then they can train the younger women to love their husbands and children, to be self-controlled and pure, to be busy at home, to be kind, and to be subject to their husbands, so that no one will malign the word of God. Similarly, encourage the young men to be self-controlled. In everything set them an example by doing what is good. In your teaching show integrity, seriousness and soundness of speech that cannot be condemned, so that those who oppose you may be ashamed because they have nothing bad to say about us (Titus 2:1-8).

Self-control is a fruit of the Spirit, and the primary instruction to both the husband and the wife is to have godly character. It is not hard for a woman to be subject to a man of character who is in subjection to God.

Submitting to Authority

Being under authority is for our own protection. "Everyone must submit himself to the governing authorities, for there is no authority except that which God has established. The authorities that exist have been established by God. Consequently, he who rebels against the authority is rebelling against what God has instituted, and those who do so will bring judgment on themselves" (Rom. 13:1-3).

I knew a Christian leader who was verbally critical of everybody he was supposed to be submissive to—his pastor, his employer, his governor and his president. He couldn't understand why all of his children were rebellious. Ironically, I'm sure he never even considered himself to be rebellious. Like many, he would go to church and critique the message and criticize the music. Yet we are not supposed to sit in judgment of the message—the message sits in judgment of us. We should enter into the experience of worship rather than sit outside acting like critics. Scripture requires us to submit to and pray for all those who are in authority over us.

I have also known wives who believe they were born to rule. They marry some spineless mouse who wouldn't dare stand in their way. One such woman brought her pathetic husband to see me about their college-aged daughter. The mother didn't like her daughter's boy-friend (I didn't either, for that matter). I listened politely for an hour as this woman described her marriage and her family. Several times, she made a point of saying she didn't want to be the head of her home. Finally, she ran out of steam and, to my surprise, asked, "We have been together for an hour now; what do you think of me?" I said, "Mrs. Apple Blossom, you have said you don't want to be the head of your home three times, but you have spoken a thousand words to your husband's one. What do you want me to believe?"

The daughter's choice for a boyfriend was not good, but why did she choose him? Her choice had been deeply affected by the conflict she had to live with at home and the role reversal she had witnessed in her parent's relationship. Her boyfriend was the exact opposite of her father. He took charge and ran the show, but not in a godly way.

Trusting God to work in our lives through less-than-perfect government officials, employers, husbands and parents requires great faith. Yet every biblical instruction to submit to governing officials is accompanied by a promise for us. Sometimes, however, we must obey God rather than man. For instance, people who issue commands or directives outside the realm of their authority do not have to be obeyed. Authority figures who issue commands that morally contradict God's Word do not have to be obeyed. Others in authority who violate their responsibilities through abusive behavior should also be reported to the governing authorities of the land that have been established to protect the innocent.

On the other hand, refusing to be submissive simply because we don't like our less-than-perfect authorities is also contrary to Scripture. It is rebellion, and rebellion leads to social anarchy. "Pick and choose" submission violates God's command to obey those in authority over us. With such thinking, every child could refuse to obey their parents simply because there are no perfect parents.

Iron Sharpens Iron

In Proverbs 27:15-16, after Solomon mentions the quarrelsome wife, he follows his description of her with this saying: "As iron sharpens iron, so one man sharpens another" (v. 17). Consider how iron sharpens iron. It generates a lot of heat, smoke and sparks. How can friction be avoided when a man and a woman from two different backgrounds make a commitment to live together? Conflict is inevitable. The question is, How can we handle it? Let's look at the following ways of dealing with conflict as it relates to achievement in relationships:

CONFLICT SYLE

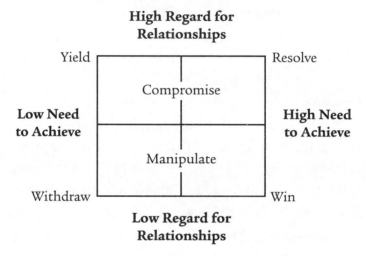

**High Regard for
Relationships**

Yield   Resolve

Compromise

**Low Need
to Achieve**   **High Need
to Achieve**

Manipulate

Withdraw   Win

**Low Regard for
Relationships**

The diagram indicates that people with a high need to achieve and little regard for relationships are likely to approach conflict with the goal of winning. If they don't care about either, they usually withdraw from any conflict. Manipulators have little or no regard for honest relationships, so they con, connive and maneuver people and circumstances to their benefit. Compromisers seek the middle ground, while those who have a high regard for relationships seek to resolve conflicts when they believe something can be accomplished by confrontation. If it isn't worth the effort to seek resolution, they yield to keep the peace.

No single correct way exists to approach every conflict. If we attend a function where a fight is about to erupt and nobody wants to establish any meaningful relationships, the best course of action is to withdraw. Other situations call for us to win, such as making a stand for righteousness' sake. However, I can't think of any situation in which we should resort to manipulation.

Conflict is an inevitable part of life, and we have all adopted styles for dealing with it. Before their conversions, Paul and Peter would probably have sought winning. They were both high achievers. Before Paul could become a reconciler, God had to strike him down, and Peter had to be humbled by denying Christ. Judas was a manipulator. Barnabas would likely yield during a conflict, and John would probably compromise to keep the peace. Compromise is not a dirty word when it is related to living with others. It only becomes wrong when we compromise our identities as God's children and our beliefs in the truth of His Word.

Who are the most insecure in their response to dealing with conflict? Those who routinely withdraw, manipulate or strive to win. The basis for a true sense of security consists of deep meaningful relationships. People who have meaningful relationships are far more secure than those who need to win or always be right.

How many verses in the Bible say we have to be right or win in every circumstance? How many verses in the Bible require us to be loving, kind, merciful, patient, forgiving, accepting and gentle? When the price for winning costs us meaningful relationships, the price is too high. Yielding or compromising to keep the peace when something can be resolved will also be costly in the long run. We can sweep issues under the carpet for a time, but eventually we will trip over them. The goal is to resolve conflicts, not just manage them.

Dealing with Conflicts

Husbands and wives have different experiences, interests, concerns and perspectives when it comes to resolving conflicts. The best opportunity for resolving the conflict emerges when both perspectives are heard and appreciated. By entertaining diverse ideas and perspectives, we have the potential to unearth more alternatives.

Conflicts handled incorrectly can lead to stalemates rather than decisions and ultimately damage our relationships. Whether the conflict is constructive or destructive will be determined as follows:

Destructive When:	Constructive When:
Spouses do not understand the value of conflict that naturally comes when other opinions and perspectives are shared.	Spouses understand the need to hear the other side so that responsible decisions can be made.
There is a competitive climate that implies a win-lose situation.	There is a cooperative spirit and commitment to the marriage that searches for a win-win situation.
"Getting my own way" is all important.	Doing it God's way is all important.
Spouses employ all kinds of defense mechanisms, including projection, suppression, blame, withdrawal and aggression.	Spouses aren't defensive and assume that disagreements evolve from the other person's sincere concern for the marriage.
Spouses are locked into their own viewpoints, unwilling to consider the perspective and ideas of their mates.	Spouses believe they will eventually come to an agreement that is better than any one individual's suggestion.
Spouses resort to personal attacks instead of focusing on the issues.	Disagreements are confined to issues rather than personalities.
Personal ideas and opinions are valued over the marriage.	The marriage relationship is more important than the need to win or to be right.

Communication Styles

Destructive relationships perpetuate cliques, subgrouping, deadlocks, stalemates and tension. Couples within these settings live with many unresolved personal conflicts. Such personal conflicts must be resolved before healthy decisions can be made. Constructive conflict resolution results in unity and a high level of trust. Sharing between spouses is open and honest.

When couples or families attempt to resolve their conflicts, it is not necessary to agree with everything everyone else says. Instead, it is important for all parties to have an equal opportunity to express their views and share their feelings. Fathers or husbands will ultimately be responsible for the final decision. Wise fathers make decisions only after they have heard all the facts and humbled themselves before God. Often the final decision will be, "You're right, honey. Let's do it the way you suggested." Sometimes the decision is, "You were right, son, and I was wrong."

The three criteria for successful conflict resolution are (1) the grace of God, (2) care and concern for one another, and (3) the ability to mutually communicate. Let's look at possible styles of communication as they relate to relationships and achievement:

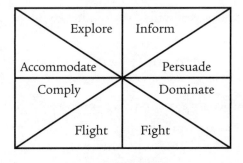

**High Regard for
Relationships**

	Explore	Inform	
Accommodate		Persuade	
Comply		Dominate	
	Flight	Fight	

**Low Need
to Achieve**

**High Need
to Achieve**

**Low Regard for
Relationships**

People with a high need to achieve tend to control the conversation. If they have a higher regard for relationships, they will try to persuade the other person. If they don't care or value relationships, they will tend to dominate. With this style, one person assumes the primary role, and the conversation is usually one-way. On the other extreme, people who have a low need to achieve tend to relinquish control of the conversation to the other person. Their style is to accommodate and comply. They are usually quite receptive to others. They prefer to stay in the background and shift the responsibility for conversation to others.

People who have little regard for relationships tend to fight if they want to achieve something or flee if they don't. Such people generally avoid contact with others. They block communication by neither soliciting nor contributing to the conversation. On the other extreme, people who have a high regard for relationships seek to develop the relationship by adapting to the styles of informing and exploring. These styles involve mutual sharing among equals. Communication is two-way and flows back and forth between two people. Both attempt to contribute to the conversation and to understand each other.

How did we learn to communicate? The same way we learned to deal with conflict. Our parents have been our primary teachers. Their modeling was more caught than taught. Consider the following questions:

- Which conflict style typified your father, and how has it affected you?
- Which conflict style typified your mother, and how has it affected you?
- Which conflict style best typifies you?
- Which parent are you most like?
- How well did you relate to this parent as opposed to your other parent?
- Which conflict style best typifies your spouse?

Now consider how knowing these truths about yourself and your spouse affects your relationship.

Group Discussion

	Agree	Disagree
1. Some things are better left unsaid, even if your spouse insists on knowing.	___	___
2. Quarreling is always wrong in a marriage relationship.	___	___
3. Spouses should be able to discuss their marital problems with their best friends.	___	___
4. Only positive feelings should be expressed in a marriage relationship.	___	___
5. The husband should always make the final decisions.	___	___
6. Speaking the truth in love doesn't mean you always have to tell the truth.	___	___
7. If you become very angry, the best thing to do is to walk away.	___	___
8. A good fight now and then makes for a better marriage.	___	___
9. The wife should tell her husband when she wants sex because he is always ready.	___	___
10. The husband should have control of the finances in the home.	___	___
11. You don't have to forgive each other if the other person won't admit he or she is wrong.	___	___
12. Wives are actually in a better position to make decisions concerning the family.	___	___
13. A husband and wife should always sleep in the same bed.	___	___

	Agree	Disagree
14. There should be no secrets between the husband and the wife.	___	___
15. The husband should stay out of the kitchen.	___	___
16. The father should lead the family devotions.	___	___
17. It is okay to go into debt if the family will benefit from it.	___	___
18. A husband should trust his wife's discernment.	___	___
19. A husband should always tell his wife where he is going and for how long.	___	___
20. The authors should never have suggested we discuss these issues with our spouses present.	___	___

Devotional Guide for Couples

Read Ephesians 4:15,25-32 and discuss the value of speaking the truth to one another in love and the damage done when unwholesome words are used.

CREATED MALE, CREATED FEMALE

*So God created man in his own image, in the image of God
he created him; male and female he created them.*

GENESIS 1:27

*There is neither Jew nor Greek, slave nor free, male nor female,
for you are all one in Christ Jesus.*

GALATIANS 3:28

My wife, Nancy, and I (Chuck) were on vacation in Maui, Hawaii, celebrating our thirteenth wedding anniversary. Each morning, we sat on the second-story deck of our condo and read, prayed, sipped tea and soaked up the sun while watching two small birds build their nest in a tree just a few feet away.

It's amazing how God builds the principles of cooperation and teamwork into His creation. The male (identified by his markings) was the supplier, bringing in the resources—strands of plants about six inches to a foot long. The female was the architect and builder, working steadily inside a covered nest that kept her hidden from view most of the time. But the shaking, pulling and weaving made her industrious presence obvious.

A couple of times, intruders threatened. The male flew into action—diving, harassing and attacking. He made life so miserable for any bird (no matter how large) that came near his nest that it simply chose to go elsewhere. Call him protective, possessive or jealous if you like, but this little male was defending his home and his family.

Watching how this industrious male handled failure and success was interesting. When he dropped a strand to the ground below, an obvious failure, he looked and looked for it but never recovered it. Then he rested for a while. He didn't work more frantically to try to make up for it. Instead, he just rested and recovered his senses. After a success, however (sticking a strand into the nest where the female would pull it inside and weave it into a beautiful place), he quickly flew off for another strand.

It was success upon success, resource upon resource. Every success led quickly to another and then another.

Meanwhile, the skillful female was designing and building a home for her future young. Through her careful efforts, the nest took shape strand by strand, day by day. When finished, the fully enclosed nest provided shelter, protection and privacy. It was well anchored so that the high winds would not blow it down.

The pair of nest builders provided a living parable right before our eyes. They provided a wonderful picture of what happens in a good marriage:

- Efficiency through division of labor
- Resting after failure
- Working hard until success comes
- Defending home and family
- Providing resources hour after hour, day after day
- Creating design and beauty
- Furnishing shelter, protection and privacy
- Preparing diligently for the future

Building a great marriage and family requires these nest-building principles in action. In Genesis, God gives the role of "suitable helper" to Eve and, by implication, to all wives (see Gen. 2:18,20-24). She complements and completes him. In the New Testament, God gives the husband the same role in the family as Christ has in the Church, namely as the "head" (see Eph. 5:23). The husband is to think ahead on her behalf, protect her and direct the marriage for her good. He is to love his wife and sacrifice himself for her, just as Christ did for the Church. Both the husband's role as the loving, sacrificing head of his wife and the wife's role of a suitable helper who complements and completes her husband are biblical—and practical. Let's learn from the Creator. He knows how marriage is supposed to be done!

Subtle Differences

Christ not only loves the Church but also understands it completely. With the human limitations of maleness and femaleness, it can sometimes be hard for us to fully understand each other. How can any husband serve as the Christlike head of his wife without growing in his understanding of her? How can any wife give godly submission to her husband without growing in her understanding of him? It is natural to think our spouses are just like us, even though we inherently know better. When we grasp the subtle differences between men and women, we just might gain new insights into our biblical roles as wives and husbands.

Both men and women were created in the image of God, but they were created *male* and *female* (see Gen. 1:27). I recall teaching a small child how to identify men and women. Daddy was a man; Mommy was a woman. His brother was a man; his sister was a woman. (We're keeping it simple here!) In about 10 minutes, he understood how to identify every person he met as male or female.

The subtle differences that extend far beyond physical characteristics are not so obvious. Men and women have different ways of seeing the world, different styles of communicating, and different methods for coping with stress. However, by sharing a few examples in this chapter, we hope you will gain a greater appreciation for the way God designed His children as male and female.

Please understand that individuals vary more among themselves because of personality and character differences than because of their sex. Your spouse may not be at all like the men or women described in this chapter, yet these generalities will provide you with clues to help you understand your mate. The purpose here is to get a better understanding of how your spouse is different from you, and vice versa.

Worldview

Men and women vary in how they see the world and their roles in it. Men see the world as a race, a war, a hunt. Their job is to achieve, to produce and to succeed. Like the male nest builder, men see themselves as runners, warriors and providers. Men feel driven to generate, fabricate and procreate. Ask most men who they are, and they will usually respond in terms of their occupations: "I am a teacher, an electrician, an engineer." They may care deeply for their families—as intensely as their wives do— but in their souls, men long to achieve, to succeed, to win. God created them male.

Women see the world as a family, a nest, a place of beauty. Their job is to nurture, to care and to shelter. Like the female nest builder, women see themselves as settlers, peacemakers and designers. They feel driven to relate, associate and cultivate. Ask most women who they are and they will often respond in terms of their relationships: "I'm a friend of . . . the wife of . . . the mother of . . ." Women may succeed in their careers—and outdo their male competitors—but in their souls they long for friendships, family, children and home. God created them female.

My caring wife, Nancy, discovered a moving description of this passion that women have for family and relationship. It's called "What Motherhood Really Means."

> Time is running out for my friend. While we are sitting at lunch, she casually mentions that she and her husband are thinking of "starting a family." What she means is that her biological clock has begun its countdown, and she is being forced to consider the prospect of motherhood.

"We're taking a survey," she says, half joking. "Do you think I should have a baby?"

"It will change your life," I say carefully, keeping my tone neutral.

"I know," she says. "No more sleeping in on Saturdays, no more spontaneous vacations . . ."

But that is not what I mean at all. I try to decide what to tell her.

I want her to know what she will never learn in childbirth classes. I want to tell her that the physical wounds of childbearing heal, but that becoming a mother will leave an emotional wound so raw that she will be forever vulnerable.

I consider warning her that she will never read a newspaper again without asking, "What if that had been my child?" That every plane crash, every fire will haunt her. That when she sees pictures of starving children, she will look at the mothers and wonder if anything could be worse than watching your child die.

I look at her carefully manicured nails and stylish suit and think that no matter how sophisticated she is, becoming a mother will reduce her to the primitive level of a she-bear protecting her cub. That an urgent call of "Mom!" will cause her to drop her best crystal without a moment's hesitation.

I feel I should warn her that no matter how many years she has invested in her career, she will be professionally derailed by motherhood. She might arrange for childcare, but one day she will be going into an important business meeting, and she will think about her baby's sweet smell. She will have to use every ounce of discipline to keep from running home, just to make sure her child is all right.

I want my friend to know that everyday decisions will no longer be routine. That a five-year-old boy's desire to go to the men's room rather than the women's at a restaurant will become a major dilemma. That issues of independence and gender identity will be weighed against the prospect that a child molester may be lurking in the restroom. However decisive she may be at the office, she will second-guess herself constantly as a mother.

Looking at my attractive friend, I want to assure her that eventually she will shed the pounds of pregnancy, but she will never feel the same about herself. That her life, now so important, will be of less value to her once she has a child. That she would give it up in a moment to save her offspring, but will also begin to hope for more years—not to accomplish her own dreams, but to watch her child accomplish his.

My friend's relationship with her husband will change, but not in the ways she thinks. I wish she could understand how much more you can love a man who is always careful to powder the baby or who never hesitates to play with his son or daughter. I think she should know that she will fall in love with her husband again for reasons she would now find very unromantic.

I wish my modern friend could sense the bond she will feel with women throughout history who have tried desperately to stop war and prejudice and drunk driving. I hope she will understand why I can think rationally about most issues, but become temporarily insane when I discuss the threat of nuclear war to my children's future.

I want to describe to my friend the exhilaration of seeing your child learn to hit a baseball. I want to capture for her the belly laugh of a baby who is touching the soft fur of a dog for the first time. I want her to taste the joy that is so real it hurts.

My friend's quizzical look makes me realize that tears have formed in my eyes. "You'll never regret it," I say finally. Then, squeezing my friend's hand, I offer a prayer for her and me and all of the mere mortal women who stumble their way into this holiest of callings.[1]

Thank you, Dale Hanson Bourke, for a mother's view of what it means to be created female.

Dialects

Women and men vary in how they talk—in their dialects. Watch small children interact and you will soon discover that girls are more verbal and have larger vocabularies than boys. Boys make more action noises—*brmmm, eeeoow, whoooow*—and have smaller vocabularies than girls.

Adult women tend to share feelings with a bent toward drama. Men tend to share information with a bent toward problem solving. Women thrive on communication; men thrive on action (even watching it on TV). In marriage, women desire to maintain verbal relationships with their husbands, no matter how much time it takes. In marriage, men desire companionship in recreation, social activities and church functions, no matter how inconvenient the timing.

Men prefer facts; women prefer feelings. Recently, I was waiting in the Portland, Oregon, airport when I overheard a couple talking with a friend. I noticed with interest that they were both talking at the same time! The man was giving information about the letter he would write tomorrow. The woman was sharing her complaint about the postal service. She was telling about a friend who had mailed two letters to the same city at the same time. One had arrived in a single day; the other had arrived a week later. Both the husband and wife kept talking nonstop. He spoke a male dialect—"just the facts" and she spoke a female dialect—"Let me tell you how I feel."

Women and men also vary in their choice of topics for conversation. Simply contrast women's magazines with men's magazines. A humorous example came from the first Promise Keepers Conference in Anaheim,

California, in May 1994. A delightful moment in the conference occurred when a Promise Keepers staff member's wife sent a note to be read from the platform. She suggested (tongue in cheek) that the topics these men were considering were far too inadequate. Instead, she made some creative suggestions.

- PMS—How to Keep Your Mouth Shut
- Why a Vacuum Cleaner Is Not a Good Birthday Present
- Parenting Does Not End at Conception
- The Male Ego—God's Little Joke

Although her suggestions were intended to be humorous, please note something: All of her topics were relationship oriented. God created her female.

Sexuality

Men and women vary in understanding their sexuality. Men see sex primarily as a physical act. Women see sex primarily as an emotional relationship. Sexual attraction for men begins with the "eye gate." A beautiful woman raises his physical voltage. Sexual attraction for women begins with the "ear gate." A man with a gift for tender talk raises her emotional voltage.

A man's sexual desire is often impulsive. He responds to an attractive woman—or the image of one—and his desire is aroused. It makes no difference at first whether or not he even knows her. A woman's sexual desire is often selective. She responds to a particular man, to his caring ways, his attentiveness, his personality, his words and especially the awareness that he finds her attractive. These qualities make the difference in whether she knows him or would like to know him.

Take a look at male lust and female lust after the Fall and sin's entrance into the world. The differences highlight the evil ways that men and women pervert sexual desire. In our culture, the epitome of male lust is pornography. It is full of nudity, exploitation, copulation and rape. Women are less likely to be addicted to pornography. In our culture, the epitome of female lust is the TV soap opera. It is full of drama, romance, intrigue and adultery. Seldom is a man addicted to soap operas. Male lust is impersonal; female lust is intensely personal. Male lust tends to conquer and exploit; female lust tends to captivate and control.

Men need sex in order to feel love.[2] The act of sex itself puts a man in touch with his feelings of emotional love for a woman. For years as a pastor, I counseled wives in troubled marriages to increase the frequency of intercourse and to take the initiative in doing so. It was a shortcut to opening their husbands up to feelings, conversation and, sometimes, even church attendance. When men's sexual needs are satisfied, they become more open, tender and ready to deal with communication problems and marriage-related difficulties. Their interest in the marital relationship increases.

Women need to feel loved in order to have sex. They need communication and understanding first. They need relaxation and to feel they are in a great relationship in order to enjoy sex fully. They need commitment, love and understanding to release their sensual side to their husbands and the passion that accompanies it.

It took Neil and me far too long to discover these basic realities about our own wives. Taking time to listen, to empathize and to understand was a big part of loving our wives in the way they wanted to be loved. When the Bible says, "Husbands, love your wives, just as Christ loved the church and gave himself up for her" (Eph. 5:25), it certainly includes sacrificing our own preferences for their good. That includes restraining our passions so that our total relationship can benefit in the long run.

Stress

Men and women vary in the way they handle stress. Men will take time out to be alone, no matter whom they may hurt in the process. They will fight for their "freedom." Women will find time to share their feelings, whether or not their husbands will listen. They will fight for some understanding of their emotional ups and downs.

Men have a tendency to go away into their own private caves at times. They simply walk out on the women (and others) in their lives and hibernate for an hour or two, or even a day or two. It's typical of men . . . and women seldom understand it.[3]

Understanding Men and Caves

What frustrates wives is that men seldom if ever explain what they are doing or why. They just disappear, walk out, leave the room or the house. When they come back, usually in a good mood and ready to talk, they have no idea why the women in their lives seem upset.

When men enter their caves, they are anchoring their souls. They isolate to find the solutions to their problems or to gain a new perspectives on life. When men spend all their spare time with their wives or with other men, they lose a valuable part of themselves. They can't explain it, but it's gone. Troubles begin to bother them; they feel irritable; little things don't make sense. Men need time to sort things out, think things over and commune with God.

Not all caves are the same. Some men (the famous "couch potatoes") use the TV. Some go hunting or fishing, often alone. Some become engrossed in a hobby or their career. Some just go for a drive or for a walk or somewhere to be alone. Some go to their offices, their computers or their places of prayer. But they walk away, and their wives are usually left feeling rejected and misunderstood.

Two helpful tips for understanding caves can make all the difference in marriage. One is for husbands, the other is for wives. For husbands, the magic words are, "I'll be back" or "I'll be right back." Men don't have a clue how much reassurance these words provide for their wives when they walk out. She feels valued because he acknowledges her, secure because he commits himself to her again, and safe because he reassures her that he is not leaving for good.

For women, the helpful tip is to do something enjoyable while he is hibernating. Wives should never, ever follow a man into his cave. A man going into his cave is like a frustrated bear seeking hibernation or a dragon spitting fire. Following a man into his cave is a sure way to get clawed or burned. Leave him alone, and he will come home wagging his tail behind him, usually happy and at peace with himself and with you! While you wait for him, phone a female friend, go shopping, enjoy a hobby, read a good book or magazine. Do something you want to do and thoroughly enjoy it.

Men are more ready to talk, communicate and be decent human beings when they come out of their caves. If they are Christians, they may have met with God during this time, or at least relaxed and rested. If they are not, they are still men and will have found something within themselves that makes them more whole, more fun, more enjoyable to live with.

Wives, give men the freedom they desire at moments when they desperately need it. Then capitalize on the communication time when they come out of their caves. Husbands, give women the reassurance that retreating to the cave is normal, that it's not their fault, and that you will be back. Putting these insights into practice can help make your marriage better.

Gaining Insight into Women and Waves

Men fight for the freedom to be alone; women care intensely about their feelings. They also want their men to understand and care. Like waves in the ocean, women's feelings about themselves—and about life in general—ebb and flow. The wave builds to a peak, and then subsides. The cascading of the wave gains momentum, and then tumbles toward shore.

God pronounced His creation of women as very good. He has a purpose for the ebb and flow of their emotional experiences. These waves cleanse the inner stains and wrinkles in their souls with their emotional descent and ascent.

As each new wave rises, women feel better, renewed, reinvigorated. Christian women feel closer to the Lord Jesus and to their families than before. Even non-Christian women feel emotionally released and recharged. It's all part of being created female, and men (especially husbands) need to understand it.

Men, in general, and husbands, in particular, can foul up this God-given rhythm in women's lives. If they don't understand waves, they often react incorrectly. They try to stop the cascading by fixing the problem, denying women's feelings or taking it all personally. Many husbands try to change their wives when they begin an emotional descent—or they simply give up and walk away. Both reactions leave wives feeling insecure, rejected and unable to share their deepest feelings.

Disaster occurs when women stifle their God-given feelings. They remain uncleansed and plagued with inner wrinkles and blemishes. The sad result is that then they can neither love as freely nor feel as good about themselves as God intended. In cases of clinical depression (for either women or men), intense treatment is needed. Neil's "Steps to Freedom in Christ" often bring about a dramatic change for the better. A support group, caring counselor and a medical exam by a competent physician may also help.

Sometimes, men feel as if they've failed as husbands when wives express their feelings. More often, they think their wives are crazy, or at least a little irrational. Men tend to react by putting up (fighting, blaming, accusing) or shutting up (running, quitting, giving up). Husbands need to train themselves to simply listen, accept and understand their wives. When they do, women can descend and ascend in their waves more easily and rapidly.

Women and waves are God-created and inevitable. When men simply love, accept and understand this, they validate their wives' feelings. Wise husbands are not personally affected by their wives' negative feelings. They don't retreat to their caves and stay there, which only makes matters worse. Wise men don't try to "fix" their wives or try to solve their wives' problems for them. Instead, they try to understand their wives' feelings. They stand by, listen attentively and give no explanations. As a result, they create a sheltered beach where waves can ebb and flow freely without restriction.

When that happens, a man sacrifices himself for his wife just as Christ does for the Church (see Eph. 5:23-28). He goes all out in his love for her, allowing God to release her inner radiance. It's beauty treatment for the soul. (Women, when we men fail miserably, as we often do, turn to your women friends and to the Lord Himself. They understand!)

The list of male and female differences is endless. The point is that we need to understand that our spouse sees life, approaches life and handles life differently from the way that we do. God knew what He was doing when He made men and women different, and yet we are one in Christ. The differences make up much of the magnetism that draws men and women together in marriage.

We must never use our maleness or femaleness as an excuse for taking advantage of the other. Instead, we should use our uniqueness to meet one another's needs, help each other and encourage each other. The better we understand our differences, the more we will appreciate each other's strengths. We should rejoice that we were created male or created female and rejoice that our spouse complements us.

Notes

1 Adapted from Dale Hanson Bourke, *Everyday Miracles, Holy Moments in a Mother's Day* (Dallas: Word Publishing, 1989), pp. 1-4. Used by permission.

2. John Gray, *Mars and Venus in the Bedroom: A Guide to Lasting Romance and Passion* (New York: Harper Collins Publishers, 1995), pp. 1-6.

3. John Gray, *Men Are from Mars, Women Are from Venus: A Practical Guide for Improving Communication and Getting What You Want in Your Relationships* (New York: Harper Collins Publishers, 1992), pp. 30-35.

Group Discussion

1. Share some examples of how men and women view life differently.

2. How are motherhood and fatherhood different?

3. In what ways do men and women communicate differently?

4. What are some common caves that men have?

5. How do women live out their emotional waves?

6. What can happen when we fail to understand our spouse?

Devotional Guide for Couples

Read Proverbs 3:13-20 and ask God for guidance and wisdom in understanding your spouse. Then, based on what you have learned in this chapter, share with your spouse what you want him or her to know about you and explain why you do what you do in certain circumstances.

PUTTING CHRIST FIRST

Do not suppose that I have come to bring peace to the earth. I did not come to bring peace, but a sword. For I have come to turn "A man against his father, a daughter against her mother, a daughter-in-law against her mother-in-law— a man's enemies will be the members of his own household."
Anyone who loves his father or mother more than me is not worthy of me; anyone who loves his son or daughter more than me is not worthy of me; and anyone who does not take his cross and follow me is not worthy of me. Whoever finds his life will lose it, and whoever loses his life for my sake will find it.

MATTHEW 10:34-39

A House Divided

When I (Neil) pastored a church, an elderly couple sought my advice about their daughter. She had made a decision for Christ early on and had been active in church during her youth. Then she met a man who was not a Christian and married him without her parents' consent. About every six months, I would see their daughter in church alone. Estranged from her parents and struggling in her marriage, she would stop by my office or give me a call to ask for prayer or advice. Finally, the marriage ended in divorce.

The parents' uncompromising commitment to Christ, the daughter's halfhearted commitment to Christ, and her husband's non-commitment to Christ became the sword that cut them apart. After the divorce, this young woman shared with me how she had planned to "save" the marriage. She had believed that if she was submissive and went along with her husband to the bars and did whatever he wanted her to do, eventually she could win him over. "I thought it was the only way to keep the peace," she said.

In all my years of ministry, I have never heard of a situation in which this approach worked. But I have heard many testimonies about how non-Christian spouses were won over by their marriage partners who would not compromise their commitment to Christ, while faithfully assuming the responsibility in their marriages to love, accept and respect their spouses. How can non-Christian spouses respect their Christian mates if they are not living what they profess to believe?

In the opening passage from Matthew 10:34-39, there is no mention made of bringing a sword between the husband and the wife. The conflict is between family members. The truth being driven home early in the Gospels is that the family is not the primary focus of God's salvation. He came to save individuals, not marriages. Helping a couple get along at the expense of either spouse's salvation is not God's plan.

When I worked as an engineer, I knew a coworker who was separated from his spouse. All attempts at reconciliation proved futile. Finally, they divorced. Both started searching for something in life that would give them meaning. Unbeknown to each other, and in totally unrelated experiences, they both found the Lord. Six months later, the young wife mysteriously died. Had the Lord used the separation, knowing that she had a terminal illness, to bring her to salvation before she died?

God places neither family nor even marriage first. Rather, it is God who is first and foremost. Why? Doesn't God care about our marriages and our families? Of course He does. The family is the first institution He created. But the whole can be no greater than the sum of its parts. A chain is no stronger than its weakest link. The measure of a marriage is the maturity of both the husband and the wife. The order of Scripture is to first present every person complete in Christ (see Col. 1:28), so our marriages and our families can be whole and functional again in Christ.

Fallen Nature

The Old Testament era ended on a sour note, and the New Testament begins no better. The Lord's chosen people were in political bondage to Rome and in spiritual bondage to an apostate Sanhedrin and the god of this world, Satan. The glory had departed from the nation of Israel, but a faithful remnant remained, and the seed of Abraham (see Gal. 3:16) was about to make His entrance: "The Word became flesh and made his dwelling among us. We have seen his glory, the glory of the

One and Only, who came from the Father, full of grace and truth" (John 1:14). The blessing of Abraham was about to be extended to all nations of the world (see Gen. 12:3).

Throughout the Old Testament, nothing had changed about the basic nature of fallen humanity. "The intent of man's heart is evil from his youth" (Gen. 8:21, *NASB*). Jeremiah says, "The heart is deceitful above all things and beyond cure" (17:9). The law had done nothing to change this. "For if a law had been given that could impart life, then righteousness would certainly have come by the law. But the Scripture declares that the whole world is a prisoner of sin" (Gal. 3:21-22). Telling people that what they are doing is wrong does not give them the power to stop doing it, because the law is powerless to give life (see Rom. 8:3,13).

Even more discouraging is the statement by Paul that "the sinful passions aroused by the law were at work in our bodies" (Rom. 7:5). The law actually has the capacity to stimulate what it is trying to prohibit. If you don't believe that is true, try telling your children that they can go "here," but they can't go "there." The moment you say that, where do they want to go? They want to go "there." They probably didn't even want to go there until you said they couldn't.

I don't know why the forbidden fruit is more desirable, but it certainly seems to be. That is why portions of Romans 7 and Galatians 3 are written to correct the wrong conclusion that the law is sinful. Laying down the law, however, will not resolve sinful passions or resolve marital conflicts. The core problem is the basic nature of humanity, not its behavior. That is why marriage counseling that attempts to shape only the behavior of either spouse is so unfruitful.

The Pharisees were the moral perfectionists (legalists) of their day. But Jesus said, "For I tell you that unless your righteousness surpasses that of the Pharisees and the teachers of the law, you will certainly not enter the kingdom of heaven" (Matt. 5:20). In the Sermon on the Mount, Jesus confronts the issue of genuine righteousness, which is determined by the condition of the heart. For instance, He says, "You have heard that it was said, 'Do not commit adultery.' But I tell you that anyone who looks at a woman lustfully has already committed adultery with her in his heart" (vv. 27-28). Although it isn't committing adultery to "look," looking is the evidence that adultery has already been committed in the heart.

Jesus goes on to say, "If your right eye causes you to sin, gouge it out" or "If your right hand causes you to sin, cut it off and throw it away" (vv. 29-30). Does your eye or hand cause you to sin? I don't think so. If we kept cutting off body parts to keep us from sinning, we would end up being nothing more than dismembered torsos rolling up and down the aisles of our churches!

Some see this passage as an admonition to take whatever drastic means are required to stop sinning, thus emphasizing the hideousness of sin. In actuality, it would be better to be dismembered than to spend eternity apart from Christ, but I don't think that is the point Jesus is trying to make. Taking cold showers to put out the fires of passion and walking blindfolded on a sunbathers' beach may bring temporary relief, but such measures do not deal with the condition of the heart. Such behavior would be necessary if the only option we had was to live under the law, but Jesus is making the case for genuine righteousness, which is to change the nature of the heart.

To further illustrate, Jesus continues, "It has been said, 'Anyone who divorces his wife must give her a certificate of divorce.' But I tell you that anyone who divorces his wife, except for marital unfaithfulness, causes her to become an adulteress, and anyone who marries the divorced woman commits adultery" (vv. 31-32). Apparently, the religious leaders had adulterous hearts. Therefore, to get around the law, they simply gave their wives a certificate of divorce. The certificates supposedly freed them to marry the ones they desired in their hearts, without breaking the law. Jesus said they didn't have legitimate grounds for divorce, so instead of avoiding adultery, they were actually propagating it.

Trying to live a righteous life externally when we are not righteous internally will only result in our being "whitewashed tombs, which look beautiful on the outside but on the inside are full of dead men's bones and everything unclean" (Matt. 23:27). It is not what goes into a person that defiles him or her, but what comes out (see Mark 7:15). "For from within, out of men's hearts, come evil thoughts, sexual immorality, theft, murder, adultery, greed, malice, deceit, lewdness, envy, slander, arrogance and folly. All these evils come from inside and make a man 'unclean'" (Mark 7:21-23).

A New Nature

"The reason the Son of God appeared was to destroy the devil's work. No one who is born of God will continue to sin, because God's seed remains in him" (1 John 3:8-9). No two verses in the Bible capture more succinctly what must happen for us to live a righteous life in Christ. Our basic nature has to be changed, and we need to have a means by which we can overcome the evil one. We "were by nature children of wrath" (Eph. 2:3, *NASB*). "You were once darkness, but now you are light in the Lord. Live as children of light" (Eph. 5:8). Only God can change who we are. It is our responsibility to believe the truth and change how we live.

In the last chapter of the Old Testament, the prophet Malachi wrote, "He will turn the hearts of the fathers to their children, and the hearts of the children to their fathers" (Mal. 4:6). Malachi prophesied that the hearts of the fathers and the hearts of the children would be turned. Arranging family programs and special events without a change of hearts will probably not accomplish much. Being alive and free in Christ is the only means by which our hearts can be truly changed.

We were born dead (spiritually) in our trespasses and sins (see Eph. 2:1). Jesus came to give us life—the same life that Adam and Eve lost when they sinned. Many of us have been presented the idea that Jesus was the Messiah who came to die for our sins and, if we believe in Him, we will be forgiven and go to heaven when we die. What's wrong with this teaching?

First, it gives the impression that eternal life is something we get when we die, which isn't true. "He who has the Son has life; he who does not have the Son of God does not have life" (1 John 5:12). Every child of God is alive in Christ right now. "For he has rescued us from the dominion of darkness and brought us into the kingdom of the Son he loves, in whom we have redemption, the forgiveness of sins" (Col. 1:13-14).

Second, it is only half the gospel. If you wanted to save a dead person, what would you do? Give him life? Even if you could do that, he would only die again. To save the dead you would have to first cure the disease that caused them to die, and "the wages of sin is death" (Rom. 6:23). So, Jesus went to the cross to die for our sins. Is that the whole gospel? Absolutely not! Jesus was resurrected so that we may have life. The rest of the verse reads: "But the gift of God is eternal life in Christ Jesus our Lord" (v. 23). The fact that believers are alive in Christ is our only hope for eternity and for becoming one in Christ. "Christ in you, the hope of glory" (Col. 1:27) is the good news. Our identity and position in Christ is the basis for our victory over sin.

Because we are in Christ, we have the Spirit of God within us. Consequently, if we "walk by the Spirit, [we] will not carry out the desire of the flesh" (Gal. 5:16, *NASB*). To experience such victory, we have to renounce our self-centered and self-sufficient ways and start living in total dependence upon God. All temptation is an attempt by the evil one to get us to live our lives independently from God. Remember, apart from Christ we can do nothing of lasting significance (see John 15:5).

Only in Christ do we have the assurance that He will meet all our needs (see Phil. 4:19). Trying to resolve marital conflicts without our essential needs being met in Christ will prove counterproductive. Expecting our spouses to meet the needs in our lives that only Christ can meet will result in disappointment and heartache. Christ meets the most critical needs in our lives, which are the "being" needs. These are as follows:

Who I Am in Christ

I Am Accepted in Christ:

John 1:12	I am God's child.
John 15:15	I am Christ's friend.
Romans 5:1	I have been justified.
1 Corinthians 6:17	I am united with the Lord and one with Him in spirit.
1 Corinthians 6:20	I have been bought with a price—I belong to God.
1 Corinthians 12:27	I am a member of Christ's Body.
Ephesians 1:1	I am a saint.
Ephesians 1:5	I have been adopted as God's child.
Ephesians 2:18	I have direct access to God through the Holy Spirit.
Colossians 1:14	I have been redeemed and forgiven of all my sins.
Colossians 2:10	I am complete in Christ.

I Am Secure in Christ:

Romans 8:1-2	I am free from condemnation.
Romans 8:28	I am assured that all things work together for good.
Romans 8:33-34	I am free from any condemning charges against me.
Romans 8:35	I cannot be separated from the love of God.
2 Corinthians 1:21	I have been established, anointed and sealed by God.
Colossians 3:3	I am hidden with Christ in God.
Philippians 1:6	I am confident that the good work that God has begun in me will be perfected.
Philippians 3:20	I am a citizen of heaven.
2 Timothy 1:7	I have not been given a spirit of fear, but of power, love and a sound mind.
Hebrews 4:16	I can find grace and mercy in time of need.
1 John 5:18	I am born of God and the evil one cannot touch me.

I Am Significant in Christ:

Matthew 5:13-14	I am the salt and light of the earth.
John 15:1,5	I am a branch of the true vine, a channel of His life.
John 15:16	I have been chosen and appointed to bear fruit.
Acts 1:8	I am a personal witness of Christ's.
1 Corinthians 3:16	I am God's temple.
2 Corinthians 5:17-20	I am a minister of reconciliation.
2 Corinthians 6:1	I am God's coworker.
Ephesians 2:6	I am seated with Christ in the heavenly realm.
Ephesians 2:10	I am God's workmanship.
Ephesians 3:12	I may approach God with freedom and confidence.
Philippians 4:13	I can do all things through Christ who strengthens me.

Paul writes, "I pray also that the eyes of your heart may be enlightened in order that you may know the hope to which he has called you, the riches of his glorious inheritance in the saints, and his incomparably great power for us who believe" (Eph. 1:18-19). The problem is *not* that every child of God doesn't share in His rich inheritance or have the power to live righteously in Christ. *The problem is that we just don't see it.* "You have been given fullness in Christ, who is the head over every power and authority" (Col. 2:10). We also have authority over the evil one as long as we are strong in the Lord, because we are seated with Christ in the heavenlies (see Eph. 2:4-6).

God's Plan for Marriage

We began this book with God's plan for marriage in the Garden of Eden, a place that was not marred by sin. In 1 Thessalonians 4:3-8 (*NASB*), Paul shares God's plan for the Christian marriage in the context of a world darkened by sin:

> For this is the will of God, your sanctification; that is, that you abstain from sexual immorality [fornication]; that each of you know how to possess his own vessel in sanctification and honor, not in lustful passion, like the Gentiles who do not know God; and that no man transgress and defraud his brother in the matter because the Lord is the avenger in all these things, just as we also told you before and solemnly warned you. For God has not called us for the purpose of impurity, but in sanctification. Consequently, he who rejects this is not rejecting man but the God who gives His Holy Spirit to you.

The word "possess" in this passage of Scripture means "to acquire." It is found in the Septuagint and other literature written at the time of

Christ and refers to marrying a wife. The word "vessel" is never used anywhere else in the Bible to mean "body." In addition, the Hebrew equivalent (*keli*) of "vessel" (*skeuos*) is used in rabbinical writings concerning the wife. Thus, the passage could be translated, "That each of you know how to take a wife for himself in sanctification and honor." Even if you choose to believe that the word "vessel" refers to your own body, as the *New International Version* does, the fact remains that premarital sex is forbidden because it is counterproductive to the sanctifying process. We are to abstain from sex before marriage and sex outside of marriage because that is not the means by which we should seek a life partner. Outward appearance and sexual appeal may be what attracts us to each other, but neither has any power to sustain the relationship. That kind of attraction is like perfume. Our senses will smell it when we are putting it on, but within minutes we will not be aware of the scent.

A young couple once asked for marriage counseling because they were having marital problems. In an angry moment, the husband had told his wife that she didn't satisfy him sexually as a previous girlfriend had. In tears, she shared how hard she tried to be like that other girl, but in reality she couldn't. One day, this husband found his wife sitting on a couch with a pillow on her lap. She asked her husband if he loved her. He said he did, and she replied, "Then I'm going to make you pay for it for the rest of your life." She removed his handgun from under the pillow and shot herself in front of him.

We realize the illustration is extreme, but if we keep ourselves pure until marriage, the problem of comparison will not be a factor. Freedom from sexual comparisons is just one of many reasons why God would have us wait.

However, abstaining from immorality is not the primary focus of the 1 Thessalonians 4:3-8 passage. God views marriage in the context of sanctification; that is, the process of conforming to the image of God.

This is God's will for our lives. We will do damage to our marriages and our families if we place greater prominence on them than we do on our relationship to God. When we make our relationship with God first in our lives, we can become the spouse and the parents that God wants us to be. Nobody except us can keep that from happening.

The Work of the Cross

The central teaching of all the Gospels can be summarized with the following verse: "Anyone who does not take his cross and follow me is not worthy of me. Whoever finds his life will lose it, and whoever loses his life for my sake will find it" (Matt. 10:38-39). When we understand the truth of that passage and appropriate it, the fulfillment of the Great Commandment becomes possible: "'Love the Lord your God with all your heart and with all your soul and with all your mind.' This is the first and greatest commandment. And the second is like it: 'Love your neighbor as yourself.' All the Law and the Prophets hang on these two commandments" (22:37-40). There is only one cross, and that is the cross of Christ. We pick up that cross when we are willing to totally identify with Christ and say no to sin and self-rule.

Notice that the above verses in Matthew 10:38-39 contain a play on words. Anyone who builds his or her life around the natural order of things will lose it. In other words, if we try to find our identity and purpose in this present natural world without God, we will lose our life some day. We can't take it with us. But when we give up our self-centered, self-seeking, self-sufficient living and find our identity and freedom in Christ, we will keep our life for all eternity.

Paul said it another way: "For physical training is of some value, but godliness has value for all things, holding promise for both the present life and the life to come" (1 Tim. 4:8). It is the great ambition of fallen humanity to be happy as animals instead of being blessed as children of God. The apostle Paul doesn't say that physical discipline has no value, but it has little value compared to what can be gained by putting Christ first and living a godly life.

Being alive in Christ is the essential foundation for all that we do. Nowhere is this more important than in gaining an understanding of who we are. John says, "Yet to all who received him, to those who believed in his name, he gave the right to become children of God—children born not of natural descent, nor of human decision or a husband's will, but born of God" (John 1:12-13).

This is what breaks the curse of the Fall. We are no longer just products of our pasts. We are primarily products of the work of Christ on the cross. "Therefore, if anyone is in Christ, he is a new creation; the old has gone, the new has come" (2 Cor. 5:17). We appropriate this new life by a sincere faith in the finished work of Christ and genuine repentance. We do this first as individuals and then as couples so that the two can become one in Christ.

Knowing Who We Are in Christ

"The Spirit himself testifies with our spirit that we are God's children" (Rom. 8:16). Knowing who we are is critical, because it is impossible for us to consistently behave in ways that are inconsistent with what we believe about ourselves. It is not what we do that determines who we are—it is who we are that determines what we do. Our roles as husbands and wives do not determine who we are. We are children of God who have the responsibility to love our spouse as Christ loved the Church. Nothing has a greater impact on how we live than our relationship with God and knowing who we are in Christ.

It follows, then, that what we believe about others will have a great impact on how we relate to them. Peter admonished, "Husbands, in the same way be considerate as you live with your wives, and treat them with respect as the weaker partner and as heirs with you of the gracious gift of life, so that nothing will hinder your prayers" (1 Pet. 3:7).

Peter must have meant "weaker" in a physical strength, because any Christian woman can be as spiritually strong in Christ as any man. In fact, women are often stronger Christians than men. Thus, Peter is saying is that every husband should honor and respect his Christian wife as the child of God she really is, and vice versa. Not to do so would hinder each spouse's relationship with God. With two redeemed people married to each other, the two sides of the triangle that were broken by sin in the Fall are back in place, and the marriage is whole again.

The message in Matthew 10:34-39 cited at the beginning of this chapter raises another critical question: What happens if you try to seek self-verification and fulfillment in the world as opposed to finding it in Christ? To be somebody in this world without Christ, you would have to:

- Look good enough so that others would admire you, or
- Perform well enough so that others would applaud your accomplishments, or
- Have enough social status so that others would recognize you.

If you are more concerned about what the world says than what God says, you may be better off remaining single. After all, consider what happens to you and your spouse after you get married and start having children.

First, the house will never look as good as it did before the children arrived. You will have to baby-proof everything that is within reach of a child. Having a clean house will be a temporary state at best. You can say goodbye to your well-manicured lawn and garden. The backyard becomes your children's playpen until it rains, and then it becomes a pigpen. For women, bikinis will be out, because they will show your stretch marks. For men, the sports car will be traded in for a minivan with finger marks on every window and gum in the seats.

The family may interfere with your availability for work if you have to attend little league games and soccer practices. At work, you find yourself competing with single people or "dinks" (double income no kids) for promotions. They can work weekends when you are with your family or attending church.

Has your family ever been a social embarrassment to you or threatened your social status? For you moms, the world says that you need to get out of the house and find your "real" identity in the market place. The only way people can recognize your performance is through your career. Children only inhibit your prospects. For dads, social pressures can lead to a midlife crisis. You cannot perform or keep up with the younger generation like you used to, so you start thinking, *Maybe I need to buy a sports car that really performs, like the one that just passed my minivan.* What will happen to your public status when you're saddled with kids who won't do what they are told and a spouse who won't participate at the office party?

Remember when Jesus healed a man who was born blind? The thankful man wanted to tell everyone about Christ, but the religious establishment claimed Jesus couldn't be of God because He healed the man on the Sabbath. The blind man wouldn't recant his testimony, so the religious authorities questioned his parents. Would they stand behind the testimony of their son? No! Why not? Because the Pharisees had agreed that if anybody professed Jesus to be the Messiah, they would be thrown out of the synagogue (see John 9:22). We can't lose our social status because of our family, can we?

When we look to the world and its values for our identity and sense of worth, our family and marriage become potential enemies. However, when we look to God to discover who we are and why we are here, our marriages and families become the primary instruments God uses to conform us to His image. We will see how this works in the next chapter.

Group Discussion

1. Why is compromising our walk with God unlikely to have a positive influence on the lost?

2. How is genuine righteousness different from external conformity to the law?

3. How can legalism ruin a marriage and family?

4. How can understanding the full gospel save a family?

5. If you have not found your identity and freedom in Christ and are looking to the world for self-fulfillment and verification, how can your marriage and family seem like a liability to you?

Devotional Guide for Couples

Read Matthew 10:34-39 and discuss the implications this passage has for your marriage and family.

CONFORMING TO HIS IMAGE

*Put on the new self, which is being renewed in knowledge in the image
of its Creator. Here there is no Greek or Jew, circumcised or uncircumcised,
barbarian, Scythian, slave or free, but Christ is all, and is in all. Therefore, as
God's chosen people, holy and dearly loved, clothe yourselves with compassion,
kindness, humility, gentleness and patience. Bear with each other and forgive
whatever grievances you may have against one another. Forgive as the
Lord forgave you. And over all these virtues put on love, which binds
them all together in perfect unity.*

*Wives, submit to your husbands, as is fitting in the Lord. Husbands,
love your wives and do not be harsh with them. Children, obey your parents
in everything, for this pleases the Lord. Fathers, do not embitter
your children, or they will become discouraged.*

COLOSSIANS 3:10-14,18-21

ou better get over here; we are about to kill each other." In responding to that desperate call, I (Neil) remember thinking on the way to their house, *This is the type of call that policeman don't like to make, because families often unite against those who are trying to intervene.* The number one cause of homicide is domestic violence, and more people are injured at home than anywhere else. It can be a dangerous place to live. So I was praying that the Lord would give me wisdom.

The battle had moved to the kitchen table. As the couple hurled verbal missiles at each other, I felt like a referee at a boxing match. Their flesh was advising them to keep their guard up and do a little better at counterpunching.

They finally ran out of breath, and the fight stalled. I suggested they come up for air and go to their respective corners. The wife fixed a cup of coffee, and the husband found a pad of paper and a pencil for me to use. When they sat down again, I drew the following diagram:

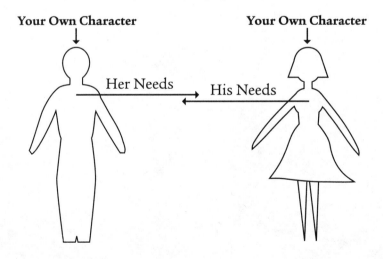

I explained that the focus of their relationship was wrong. Before God, individuals are responsible for their own character and the other person's needs. They were doing just the opposite. They were ripping the other person's character while looking out for their own needs. No relationship can survive that orientation.

What would our marriages, families and churches be like if every one of us assumed our responsibility to conform to the image of God (which is God's great goal for our lives) and committed ourselves to meet the needs of those around us (which is the essence of loving one another)? Surely that is what God has called us to be and do. Why aren't we doing it? If everybody did, we would be living in paradise.

I gave this husband and wife a piece of paper and asked them to draw a line across the middle. On the top half, they were to write down what they believed their three greatest needs were. On the bottom half, they were to write down what they thought the other person's three greatest needs were. With some effort, they were able to identify their own needs, but when it came to listing the needs of their spouse, neither had a clue. They probably had given it very little thought.

Selfishness and self-centered living will kill any marriage! Denying ourselves, picking up the cross of Christ daily and following Jesus make for a good marriage. Both husband and wife will be satisfied.

It is likely that in this case, both the husband and the wife felt so deprived of their own basic needs that they couldn't see beyond them. When people are hurting, their overwhelming thought is to stop the pain. That is why it is so important for individuals to resolve their personal and spiritual conflicts first before attempting to resolve the difficulties in their marriages. Being married does not resolve the core personal needs that can only be met in Christ. In fact, marriage has a tendency to expose character deficiencies and to reveal people's raw needs.

Another man I knew was destroying everything important to him. From his selfish perspective, everybody else was wrong: his pastor, his boss and his wife. Finally, his wife left him. Six months later, I got a call from him. He had just been released from a three-month jail sentence. He said, "This is the first time I have been clean from drugs in 10 years."

I didn't even know he had a drug problem! I asked him, "Knowing that you were losing your church, your job and your marriage, why did you continue using?"

He said, "That was the only time I ever felt good about myself."

This man didn't have to take drugs to feel good about himself. All committed Christians should feel good about themselves if they are alive and free in Christ, and living in the center of God's will (see *Overcoming a Negative Self-Image* [Regal Books]).

Common Misperceptions

Consider the following four cultural biases that mitigate Christ-centered living and oneness in marriage.

Individual Rights

The first bias is our preoccupation about individual rights. We believe in our inalienable rights and that every person should be accepted and respected for who she or he is, regardless of race, sex, social or economic status. But the balance has tipped too far if individual rights are emphasized over personal responsibilities.

Witness the pro-choice pregnant woman who publicly demands her rights over her own body while at the same time demonstrating her irresponsible use of it. We don't have an abortion problem; we have an irresponsible sex problem, and science has clearly shown that the new life within her is not part of her own body. Of course, the male counterpart is equally responsible for the misuse of his body.

We have the right to bear arms and the right to free speech, but both are deadly when misused by those who are irresponsible, self-centered and godless. The law too often deals with the effect, but not the cause. When courts hold people accountable for what is clearly their responsibility, we will see justice return to our country.

Let's apply this to marriage and family. Do I have a right as a husband to expect my wife to be submissive, or do I have a responsibility to love my wife as Christ loved the Church? Do I have a right as a parent to expect my children to obey me, or do I have a responsibility to train them in the Lord and discipline them if they are disobedient? The seeds of destruction are sown when nations, churches, families, marriages or individuals demand their rights without assuming their responsibilities.

What right do we have to expect anything from anybody else? I have no right to demand that my wife and children fulfill my expectations. I have great hopes for them. I believe in their potential, and I will do what I can to help them be all God wants them to be. But if they should fall short or deviate from my expectations, I am not disillusioned. Only God has that right, and only He has the grace to make it happen.

I help my wife and family most by assuming my responsibility to be the husband and father God wants me to be. The same is true for my wife. Her primary responsibility is to be the wife and mother God wants her to be, and nobody can keep either of us from being that. Becoming the person, parent and spouse God wants us to be is God's will for our lives.

The hurting parent may say, "You don't understand, my child is being very rebellious and I need to control him for his own good." A rebellious child cannot keep us from being the mother or father God wants us to be. The fruit of the Spirit is self-control, not child control. Our children's rebelliousness will seriously test our character, but what our rebellious children really need is for us to be the parents God wants us to be.

Our Role in Others' Lives

A second cultural bias is related to the role we play in another person's life. When our mates are not living up to our expectations or fulfilling their commitments, we are tempted to act as their consciences. However, the moment we attempt to play the role of the Holy Spirit in their lives, we misdirect their battle with God onto ourselves. We are simply inadequate for the task of playing God in someone else's life. We are supposed to "accept one another . . . just as Christ accepted [us], in order to bring praise to God" (Rom. 15:7).

How did Christ accept us? "God demonstrates his own love for us in this: While we were still sinners, Christ died for us" (Rom. 5:8). No other human factor is more important in helping others conform to the image of God than our unconditional love and acceptance.

The Difference Between Discipline and Judgment

Love and acceptance are consistent with the responsibility to discipline, but inconsistent with judging one another. Discipline is proof of our love, but at the same time we are commanded not to judge (see Matt. 7:1). Not knowing the difference between discipline and judgment is a third cultural bias.

Discipline is related to behavior, whereas judgment is related to character. We discipline those we love purely on the basis of observed behavior. Discipline must be based on what we have seen or heard. We cannot discipline someone based on hunches, guesses or intuition. Discipline is not punishment. We don't punish somebody for doing something wrong out of revenge. Rather, we discipline him or her for the purpose of superintending future choices so that person doesn't do it again. Discipline is training in righteousness. Notice how Hebrews 12:10-11 supports this:

> Our fathers disciplined us for a little while as they thought best; but God disciplines us for our good, that we may share in his holiness. No discipline seems pleasant at the time, but painful. Later on, however, it produces a harvest of righteousness and peace for those who have been trained by it.

If I catch my son telling a lie, I have a responsibility to confront him. Suppose I say, "Son, what you just said is not true!" His response may be, "You're judging me!" I am not judging him. I confronted him because of what he said, not because of who he is. But if I say, "Son, you're a liar!" that's judgment. I just attacked his character.

When discipline is appropriately administered, the situation can be resolved at the time. The offenders can confess, make retribution if called for, and be reconciled. They may have to live with the consequences of their sins, but their characters have not been impugned.

If someone attacks our character, what can we do? We can change our behavior, but we cannot instantly change our character. We can choose to change what we do, but we can't instantly change who we are. Attacking a person's character is a subtle form of rejection.

Much of what we do in the name of discipline is nothing more than character assassination. Stinging rebukes on a person's character, such as calling him or her "stupid," "clumsy," "dumb," "moron," "jerk" and "nitwit," do lasting damage to a person's sense of well-being. Name calling and labeling build walls that only forgiveness can break down.

I have seen older adults weep while forgiving their deceased parents for such verbal abuse. Any time we attack another person's character—especially our spouse's or our child's—we should confess it and ask that person for his or her forgiveness.

Half the problems in our marriages, families and ministries would disappear if we could consistently obey just one verse in the Bible: "Do not let any unwholesome talk come out of your mouths, but only what is helpful for building others up according to their needs, that it may benefit those who listen" (Eph. 4:29). The next verse says, "Do not grieve the Holy Spirit of God" (v. 30). It grieves God to see His children using their words to tear each other down. The Holy Spirit is leading us to build up one another, not put one another down.

What should we do if our spouses (or others) attack our character? Should we be defensive? Consider the example of Jesus: "When they hurled their insults at him, he did not retaliate; when he suffered, he made no threats. Instead, he entrusted himself to him who judges justly" (1 Pet. 2:23).

Those who attack the character of another are wrong to do so, and it is likely that they are people who are themselves hurting. Godly people don't attack another person's character. Defending ourselves only invites more verbal attacks. We can't let the unrighteous judgments of others determine who we are. We should entrust ourselves to Him who judges justly.

When people have unloaded their verbal guns, the last thing we want them to do is reload, and retaliating in kind gives them more ammunition. They will likely become even more adamant in their character assassinations. What happens when they have emptied their guns and we don't retaliate or defend ourselves? The Holy Spirit brings conviction on the offender, and we may be afforded an opportunity to minister to a hurting person.

Sharing Needs Appropriately

Is it appropriate to share needs with our spouses? It certainly is, but the fourth cultural bias is related to how we do it. Suppose a wife doesn't feel loved by her husband and says to him, "You don't love me anymore, do you?" Chances are he will respond by saying, "Yeah, I do." That will likely be the end of the conversation.

The wife critiqued her husband's responsibility instead of sharing her needs. Her response was a "you" judgment instead of an "I" statement. It would be better if she had said something like this: "I just don't feel loved anymore." The husband and the wife are commanded by God to love one another. So, if the spouse doesn't assume the role of the Holy Spirit, God is free to bring conviction.

Paul says, "Let our people also learn to engage in good deeds to meet pressing needs, that they may not be unfruitful" (Titus 3:14, *NASB*). The most critical needs are the being needs, which include eternal (spiritual) life, identity, acceptance, security and significance. These can only be met in Christ, yet God intended that many of our temporal needs be met through marriage and family relationships.

The capacity to meet others' needs is directly proportional to our growth in character. The more we become like Christ, the more we are able to love one another, and the home is where most of our growth and character development take place. All this is torpedoed when we stop growing and selfishly focus on our own needs at the expense of others.

Fulfilling Commitments and Relationships

God works in our lives primarily through committed relationships for two reasons. First, we cannot (or should not) run away from our commitments and responsibilities in our marriage and family relationships. This is not to say that there aren't relationships in life that we can, and in some cases should, walk away from. Scripture warns, "Do not be misled: Bad company corrupts good character" (1 Cor. 15:33).

Homes can be like pressure cookers. Trials and tribulations often are the results of living together in the confinement of our homes. But that is precisely the point, as Paul articulates in Romans 5:3-5 (*NASB*):

We also exult in our tribulations, knowing that tribulation brings about perseverance; and perseverance, proven character; and proven character, hope; and hope does not disappoint, because the love of God has been poured out within our hearts through the Holy Spirit who was given to us.

When we find ourselves in relational conflict, the flesh will often react by saying, *This job is hopeless; I better change jobs* or *This marriage is hopeless; I better get a divorce.* However, Paul says we should stay true to our commitments, honor our obligations, remain faithful to our vows, and grow up.

There are legitimate times to search for another job and seek legal separation for protection, but we need to ask the reason for leaving. Are we running away from the pressures of life instead of working through them? If so, we will be missing the primary means by which God intends to develop Christian character. Trials and tribulations reveal wrong goals in our lives, but they make possible the greatest goal, which is proven character.

How can we provide hope for a wife who has just learned that her husband left her? It is a false hope to promise that together we will win him back. We can't promise that because there are too many factors that are beyond our right or ability to control. The subtle question by some who are separated is, "How can I manipulate the other person or the circumstances so that they will have to come back?" That kind of attitude is probably why the other person left in the first place.

We offer a lot more hope if we say something like this: "If you haven't previously committed yourself to be the best possible wife and mother God wants you to be, would you now?" The best way to change a situation is to change ourselves, because that is the only thing we have the right or ability to control and change. Changing ourselves is also the best way to win back the other person. Even if that doesn't happen, we can come through the crisis of separation a better person than we were before it happened. This results in a win-win situation, because our hope lies in our own proven character.

The second reason why God works primarily through committed relationships is because they strip away our pretenses. Most of us can put on a public face and con our neighbors and casual friends, but we can't be a phony at home. Our children and spouses will see right through us. When we tell our children to behave in public, is it for their good or for us to look good? Our children know the difference. When we keep something from our spouses, they may not know *what* is wrong, but they definitely know *something* is wrong.

Our homes are fishbowls disguised as houses. When the spiritual tide is out, all the little tadpoles want to swim in their own little tide pool. But when the spiritual tide is in, they all swim harmoniously together as though somebody other than themselves were orchestrating every move. Such moments may be rare, but when they happen they are wonderful.

From Death to Life

We can see how God intends to bring us from death to spiritual life and maturity by understanding the progressive flow of the apostle Paul's message in the book of Colossians:

Chapter 1:

Verse 9	We are to be filled with the knowledge of His will in all spiritual wisdom and understanding.
Verse 13	We have been delivered out of the kingdom of darkness and transferred into the kingdom of Christ.
Verse 27	Christ in us is our hope of glory.
Verse 28	We are to present every person perfect in Christ.

Chapter 2:

Verses 6-7,10	We have been made complete *in Christ*, and are now being built up *in Him*, in order that we may walk *in Him*.
Verse 14	He canceled out our certificate of debt and nailed it to the Cross.

Verse 15	Jesus disarmed the rulers and authorities, having triumphed over them.
Verses 20-23	Legalism and personal asceticism cannot accomplish what Jesus has already accomplished.

Chapter 3:

Verse 3	We have died to who we were in Adam and are now alive in Christ.
Verses 5-9,10	We have put off the old man (self) and have put on the new self who is being renewed to a true knowledge according to the image of the One who created us.

The Lord transferred us out of the kingdom of darkness into His kingdom and made us new creations in Christ. He forgave our sins and defeated the devil. We are to put off the old self and put on the new self. After salvation, God's will for our lives is that we conform to His image. Now, refer back to the text quoted at the beginning of this chapter in Colossians 3:10-14,18-21. Notice the progressive order of our new identity in Christ, our growth in character and, finally, Paul's instructions for marriage, family and career.

Knowing Who We Are

Knowing who we are is the foundation for what we do. The barriers that separated us because of our natural heritage no longer exist: "Here there is no Greek or Jew, circumcised or uncircumcised, barbarian, Scythian, slave, or free, but Christ is all, and is in all" (Col. 3:11). In other words, for those who are in Christ, there are no racial, religious, cultural or social distinctions. Galatians 3:28 adds there are also no gender distinctions, "for you are all one in Christ Jesus." Every Christian is a child of God: "The Spirit himself testifies with our spirit that we are God's children"

(Rom. 8:16). That is how we are to perceive ourselves and other believers.

The Lord has not eradicated social order, sexual gender or lines of authority. For instance, Paul refers to slaves in Colossians 3:22, but says in verse 11 that there are no slaves. In fact, verse 11 is referring to the identity of every child of God, while verse 22 is referring to the social situation in which someone may be called to live. All Christian men, women, fathers, mothers, masters, slaves and children should live like the children of God they really are. It is not what we do that determines who we are. Who we are should determine what we do, and every believer is first and foremost a child of God.

We are all children of God living under His authority. The employee must still be submissive to the employer, the wife to her husband and the child to his or her parents. Once our identity is established, we can then grow in character. As Paul states:

> Therefore, as God's chosen people, holy and dearly loved, clothe yourselves with compassion, kindness, humility, gentleness and patience. Bear with each other and forgive whatever grievances you may have against one another. Forgive as the Lord forgave you. And over all these virtues put on love, which binds them all together in perfect unity (vv. 12-14).

These character traits are primarily developed in committed relationships. There will be harmony in our homes if we all grow together in the grace of God. Because we don't live with perfect people, the one overwhelming act of love we will repeatedly need is the grace to forgive as we have been forgiven.

Forgiveness Through *Agape* Love

When people make lists of whom they need to forgive, 95 percent of the time their own parents are the first two people mentioned. Love binds a family together, but forgiveness is the glue that holds it together. Bitterness or unresolved anger rooted in unforgiveness is the dynamite that blows marriages and families apart. Unforgiveness affords Satan an access to believers (see Matt. 18:21-35; 2 Cor. 2:10-11).

Indulging in bitterness is like swallowing poison and hoping the other person will die. Forgiving is like setting a captive free and then realizing we were the one held captive. Nothing will keep us bound to the past more than unforgiveness. If we don't forgive, Satan will destroy us. In helping others find their freedom in Christ, I have discovered that unforgiveness is the number one reason people are in bondage. In many cases, it was the only unresolved issue blocking their freedom.

Forgiving one another is the first step in loving one another. Jesus said, "A new command I give you: Love [*agape*] one another. As I have loved you, so you must love one another" (John 13:34). Why was this a new command? Weren't we always supposed to love one another? We couldn't love the unlovely before Christ because of our depraved natures.

Agape love is the love of God. We can be commanded to love others because we have become partakers of His divine nature (see 2 Pet. 1:4). God loves us not because we are lovable but because He is love. It is His nature to love us. That is why God's love for us is unconditional. God's love is not dependent on the object of love. As Jesus said, "If you love those who love you, what credit is that to you? Even 'sinners' love those who love them" (Luke 6:32). If Christian husbands or wives say they don't love their spouses anymore, they have said more about their own character than they have about their life partners. The grace of God enables us to love the unlovely.

Note also that *agape* is used in the New Testament as both a verb *and* a noun. When *agape* is used as a noun, it refers to God's character: "God is love, and the one who abides in love abides in God, and God abides in him" (1 John 4:16, *NASB*). It is the highest of all character attainments: "Love is patient, love is kind" (1 Cor. 13:4). Paul says, "The goal of our instruction is love from a pure heart and a good conscience and a sincere faith" (1 Tim. 1:5, *NASB*). Proven character, which reveals itself in the love of God, should be the goal of every Christian ministry: "By this all men will know that you are my disciples, if you love one another" (John 13:35).

When used as a verb, the love of God compels us to meet the needs of others. It has to be given away. "For God *so loved* the world that he *gave* his one and only Son, that whoever believes in him shall not perish but have eternal life" (John 3:16, emphasis added). God saw our greatest need and then, because of His love, made the ultimate sacrifice to meet it. The meaning of John 3:16 is captured in 1 John 3:16-18:

> This is how we know what love is: Jesus Christ laid down his life for us. And we ought to lay down our lives for our brothers. If anyone has material possessions and sees his brother in need but has no pity on him, how can the love of God be in him? Dear children, let us not love with words or tongue but with actions and in truth.

Those who are mature in Christ will be moved by the love of God to reach out and meet the needs of their spouses and others.

The Ruling Voice

Listen to Paul's words that are tucked between his challenge for godly character and family instruction:

> Let the peace of Christ rule in your hearts, since as members of one body you were called to peace. And be thankful. Let the word of Christ dwell in you richly as you teach and admonish one another with all wisdom, and as you sing psalms, hymns and spiritual songs with gratitude in your hearts to God (Col. 3:15-16).

The peace of Christ can rule in our hearts only if the Word of Christ richly dwells within us. The need for the Word of God to be the ruling voice in our marriage and home cannot be overemphasized. Couples and families that pray and read their Bibles together still stay together. Movies, music and magazines that are counterproductive to our Christian growth should be eliminated from the house. There are too many voices inspired by the prince of power of the air (Satan) that will turn us against God and each other. "The Spirit clearly says that in later times some will abandon the faith and follow deceiving spirits and things taught by demons" (1 Tim. 4:1).

The ruler of this world, the father of lies, will seek to destroy our life, testimony and marriage. In the high priestly prayer, Jesus says, "My prayer is not that you take them out of the world but that you protect them from the evil one. Sanctify them by the truth; your word is truth" (John 17:15,17).

The Holy Spirit is the Spirit of truth and will lead us into all truth, and that truth will set us free. We can then be the husbands and fathers, wives and mothers He has called us to be. We will sharpen each other's characters and meet one another's needs.

Group Discussion

1. What are the primary reasons why Christians aren't assuming responsibility for their own character and seeking to meet the needs of others?

2. Why is more emphasis given to human rights than to human responsibilities?

3. Explain the difference between discipline and judgment. From your own experience, how has one been helpful and the other hurtful?

4. How can you inappropriately share a need?

5. Can you explain from Scripture how and why God works through a committed relationship to build your character?

Devotional Guide for Couples

Read Ephesians 5:25-33 and Titus 2:1-5 and share with each other what you think your greatest real and felt needs are without reference to the others person's role or responsibility.

LOVE LANGUAGE

Gifts

Everyone is the friend of a man who gives gifts.

PROVERBS 19:6

Service

*Having loved his own who were in the world, he now showed them the full
extent of his love. [S]o he got up from the meal, took off his outer clothing,
and wrapped a towel around his waist. After that, he poured water into
a basin and began to wash his disciples' feet, drying them with the
towel that was wrapped around him.*

JOHN 13:1,4-5

Time

*Jacob was in love with Rachel and said, "I'll work for you seven years in return
for your younger daughter Rachel." So Jacob served seven years to get Rachel,
but they seemed like only a few days to him because of his love for her.*

GENESIS 29:18,20

Touch

How beautiful you are and how pleasing,
O love, with your delights!
Your stature is like that of the palm,
and your breasts like clusters of fruit.
I said, "I will climb the palm tree;
I will take hold of its fruit."
May your breasts be like the clusters of the vine,
the fragrance of your breath like apples,
and your mouth like the best wine.

SONG OF SONGS 7:6-9

Words

Pleasant words are a honeycomb, sweet to the soul
and healing to the bones.

PROVERBS 16:24

We have been stressing the need to know your spouse and come to terms with the personal history that everyone brings to a marriage. You really can't love someone you don't know, and misunderstanding one another is the basis for all kinds of conflicts. The point is that nobody can relate to an unknown entity. God loves us because God is love. It is His nature to love us, but He also has perfect knowledge of us and knows how to meet our needs.

Learning how to give and receive love is inextricably bound together with our ability to communicate. In his insightful book *The Five Love Languages*, Gary Chapman observes that people speak different love languages. In other words, people communicate that they love or are loved when they say or do certain things. Gary postulates that everyone has one of five primary ways of doing this:

1. Gifts
2. Service
3. Time
4. Touch
5. Words[1]

Little children seem most open to all the love languages. They squeal with delight when someone gives them *gifts*. They love Christmas and birthdays. Children naturally respond to people who *serve* them and do special things for them. They crave *time*, constantly wanting adults to

"Watch me" and take time to play with them. They love to be touched and hugged. Who gives more spontaneous and innocent hugs than little children? They give them freely and receive them with joy. They love to sit on the laps of adults who will read their favorite stories to them. Warm *words* brighten their eyes. Grandparents are usually great at giving love in all these ways.

Even children, however, seem to have a primary love language. Often, young children cannot express their love verbally, but will show it instead. Do your children constantly make you presents and love to give them to you? Gifts may be their way of showing and receiving love. Do they naturally help their brothers and sisters or always want to help you? Their love language is probably service. Do they always want your attention and want it now? They probably feel loved when you give them time and unloved if you don't. Do they climb into your lap or run to hug you often? They probably best understand love with touch or contact. Do they tell you what a good mommy or daddy you are? Love for them is most likely best expressed with words.

Preferred Love Language

Most adults have a preferred love language or a combination of two. Although we may enjoy all the languages of love, we like to receive love in one or two ways more than in others.

Most of us are not necessarily aware that our spouse's love language is different from our own. So we tend to show our love in our own language, which can lead to miscommunication or misunderstanding with our partner. The best way to discover our spouse's and our older children's love languages is simply to ask. When we learn their preferences and make the necessary adjustments, our ability to love will be greatly enhanced. After reading Gary's book, Neil and I knew our own love language and had a pretty good sense what our spouse's love language was, but we weren't sure what our children's love languages were. So we asked them, and they told us.

Neil copied the first edition of this chapter and had his family read it. On Valentines Day, they dined out and talked for hours about their love languages. Joanne's love language is time, which can often seem to be meaningless time to Neil, whose love language is service. Neil's natural bent is to serve Joanne and others by doing projects around the house and around the world. Joanne, at times, has wished he would stop and spend some time with her. To complicate matters, Neil is gone a lot of the time doing ministry.

My wife, Nancy, speaks a love language that is made up primarily of gifts and service. She frequently buys things for me. My inner response often is, *That's nice, but I really didn't need it all that much. Besides, we really can't afford it.* She was not using my love language, and I wasn't doing well at receiving hers.

Nancy is also an excellent housekeeper, well organized and constantly taking care of the little things that make life better for me. I do appreciate these acts, but I did not always think of them as expressions of love. In fact, I thought she was a little compulsive about the house and a well-organized perfectionist. I appreciated her abilities, but I didn't feel the love message on an emotional level.

Later, I learned that what really communicates love to Nancy is taking out the garbage or vacuuming the floor. To me that is slave labor, not love! But when I learned to give service freely and without grumbling, it became a love language that touched her soul. After a day off with lots of work around the house, we will often pray together in bed at night. Nancy will thank the Lord with great satisfaction for "all the things we got done that day." Her tone of voice tells me that she feels loved. I am just glad it's over and am praying silently that we will have a better day tomorrow!

My love language is made up primarily of words and touch. I like to write notes or send cards to Nancy. She always says, "Thank you. That was nice." But somehow, it doesn't cause her to turn cartwheels.

Touch is a big one for me. I can never get enough, it seems, until Nancy quietly communicates—usually not in words—"Back off. You're bugging me." Tender talk and lovemaking turn me on. My attitude is, *Who cares if we're poor or what kind of house we live in as long as we have each other?* Sorry, Charlie, but Nancy doesn't see it that way. Words and touch have their place, but real love gets practical. Opposites do attract!

When Nancy and I asked our grown children what each of them thought our love language was, they both responded, "Time." Maybe it's because I was so busy while they were growing up. Or maybe it is because their generation places a high value on friendship and spending time together. My son, Kirk, can easily spend a half hour talking on the phone to us, even if there is not much to say. At the time, my daughter, Lisa, was working in South Korea and would write to friends and family several times a week via e-mail. They are giving love in their language: time.

Showing love in the other person's language has made an enormous difference in our lives. Nancy has received some gifts that I knew she wanted. She lights up like a Christmas tree. Now, Nancy is more inclined to hug me—much to my delight! We spend all the time we can together with our children, whether in person or on the phone, and write letters to them.

Neil is learning to be less project-oriented around the house and spend more time with Joanne. He used to rush to get everything done before a big trip. Now, he tries to save the day before he leaves to just spend some time with Joanne. In the past, when he returned home from a trip, right away he would take care of all the paperwork and e-mails that had piled up. Now he postpones that for a day and takes a day off with Joanne. Joanne has learned to better appreciate the things that Neil does for her. She has come to understand that service is his primary way of showing love.

More than 20 times in the New Testament, we are instructed to give love. In fact, the command most often repeated in the New Testament is to love one another. Husbands are specifically commanded to love their wives as Christ loved the Church (see Eph. 5:25,28,33; also see Col. 3:19). *Agape*, the Greek word for love used in these passages, means that the husband is called to sacrifice his life for his wife. A small part of his sacrifice might mean learning her love language and communicating to her in that language. Learning to love is not just for men, however. Older women are also encouraged to *train* younger women to love their husbands and children (see Titus 2:4). Becoming skillful in another love language takes training!

Consider a basic truth from what Scripture does *not* say. The Bible never says anyone can demand love. Love is a command, not a demand. Nowhere does Scripture indicate love is a right rather than a responsibility. Men who demand sex and women who demand affection usually create resentment, not love. The Holy Spirit creates the fruit of self-sacrificing love: the desire to give ourselves away.

Gifts

Many cultures consider gift-giving an essential part of love and marriage. Every wedding Neil or I have conducted has included the exchange of rings as a meaningful symbol.

In *The Five Love Languages,* Gary Chapman explains that gifts need not always be expensive. They can be made or sometimes even found. Pick a wildflower and put it in a vase. Pluck a paper sack out of the trash, fold it in two, cut out a heart, write "I love you" and sign your name. Ask your spouse what kinds of gifts he or she really likes the most.[2]

For one of our anniversaries, I used the letters of the alphabet to remind myself of Nancy's outstanding character qualities. I put these in two columns, framed them, and then gave it to her. The frame was not expensive, but Nancy still keeps it displayed (where I can see it). It reads as follows:

Nancy my sweetheart,

You are everything to me. You are:

Amazing	Neat
Beautiful	One and only
Compassionate	Pure
Desirable	Quiet
Efficient	Rewarding
Fun	Steady
Gentle	Tender
Humble	Understanding
Intimate	Virtuous
Just	Wonderful
Kind	Excellent
Loving	Youthful
Merciful	Zealous

The whole alphabet can never exhaust what you mean to me!

Happy 28th Anniversary!
Your adoring husband,

Chuck

I was motivated by my love language of words and found it was a powerful way of affirming Nancy and building her up.

Personal history often affects one's ability to communicate love. A woman named Shirley once complained to her pastor that during the course of their 30-year marriage, her husband, David, had *never* given her a birthday, anniversary or even a Christmas present. When her pastor asked how that made her feel, her eyes filled with tears. She broke down and wept for several minutes, releasing years of disappointment and disillusionment. Shirley had not learned the freedom of forgiveness or the wisdom of communicating her love language to others.

The pastor could hardly believe David was so insensitive. However, when he later had an opportunity to talk with him, he soon understood David's reasons. David had grown up in a dysfunctional family in which everyone was either fighting or in a cold truce, merely tolerating each other. But on Christmas and birthdays, they went through a meaningless ritual (or so it seemed to him) of giving each other gifts. David made a foolish childhood vow that he would never give a gift just because it was expected. He would give gifts only when they really meant something. He lived by that vow.

So David brought home plenty of gifts throughout the years—gold certificates, stock options and practical presents that built financial security. Emotionally, he was a saver, not a spender, and he showed love by saving for Shirley. But David's gifts never came on birthdays, anniversaries or Christmas mornings. Worse yet, they were not the kind of gifts Shirley desired. She wanted ceramics, cards, romantic gifts— gifts that showed his tender feelings for her. She could care less about money in the bank! David thought her gift ideas were only trinkets, and not that important.

Having grown up in a poor family, David believed he was building security in ways his parents had not provided for him, but the generational sin of insensitivity to his spouse's feelings still plagued him. He had never learned to honor and value his wife's preferences and tastes. Both Shirley and David understood gifts as love language, but they totally misunderstood the other's expectations. They were communicating on different wavelengths.[3]

When we are addressing another's love language, we shouldn't guess, assume or just say, "I already know." To enjoy intimate relationships, we must ask for input, observe what is valued and learn by trial and error to discover the secret wishes of others' hearts. Then we can speak the love dialect that penetrates their souls and causes them to fall deeply in love with us. Every love language is legitimate, and the sensitive person uses all five. But the wise have leaned how best to communicate their love to others.

Service

Service was a primary way that Jesus showed His love. He said of Himself, "For even the Son of Man did not come to be served, but to serve, and to give his life as a ransom for many" (Mark 10:45). Jesus dumbfounded His disciples at the last Passover by washing their feet, a task reserved for slaves. John the beloved saw the significance. He summed it up with this caption: "Having loved his own who were in the world, he now showed them the full extent of his love" (John 13:1). Even after His resurrection and while enjoying His immortal body, Jesus cooked breakfast for the disciples (see 21:9-13).

During dating and engagement, most couples eagerly serve one another. But after a year or two of marriage, they soon revert to what they saw in their parents' homes. The generational blessings or curses are far more powerful than we realize. When we use our own love language (or our parents') instead of that of our marriage partner, we will probably be misunderstood.

Although Sue and Dan had been married for 15 years, misunderstandings between them still occurred. At a marriage retreat, they asked the guest speaker to talk to them for a few moments alone. After he asked how they showed love to each other, he received some surprising replies. Sue loved flowers and sometimes at night would put a vase with a fresh cut flower from her garden on Dan's nightstand. It was her way of telling him she might like to make love that night. However, because gifts were not David's love language, he did not get the hint. He just thought she liked flowers!

When the speaker asked David how he showed love to Sue, he told about his service on her behalf. He did the dishes, folded and put away the laundry, and tidied up the house. But as he continued talking, Sue was obviously upset. The speaker asked why she was so upset about something most wives would love.

Sue shared a story of a time when she had back surgery and was in traction, confined to bed for nearly a year. The doctors were unsure if she would ever walk again. She felt useless because her family had learned to get along without her. However, during the last 18 months she had made progress. The two things that made her feel most worthwhile were—you guessed it—doing the dishes and folding the laundry. David's use of his own love language was actually robbing Sue of feeling that he cared.[4]

Anger and criticism don't win friends and influence people, including marriage partners. Just as in dating days, love must be won, not demanded. No one ever forced anyone else to fall in love by criticizing that person or demanding love from him or her. Think back to your engagement days. What made your mate fall in love with you? The only constructive thing that criticism *can* do is help us discover our partner's love language. Both wives and husbands tend to be critical of whatever they perceive as the blockage to the love language they want to receive.

Take Mary and Mark as an example. Mary criticized Mark's hunting trips with intense hostility. He couldn't understand her feelings, because he had often hunted during their courtship. But in those days, Mark also returned home early enough to wash his truck, go over to Mary's house for dinner, and help her with projects. Now, he went hunting but did not help her with any house-related tasks. A friend exposed the problem: She did not have a problem with him hunting, but she did miss the acts of service that expressed love to her. When the service was gone, she felt unloved and ferociously criticized hunting as the hated enemy. Once each understood the other's love language and agreed to a short list of primary preferences, they found fresh hope.[5]

Another couple, Dean and Kris, were moving to another state. Before they left, they asked for some counsel from Patti, a respected friend. Patti shared the love language concept. Kris told Dean she really wanted him to hold her often and tell her he loved her. Because he had previously been involved in affairs, she needed his reassurance. Dean said he could do that. When asked what he wanted, Dean said he would appreciate having the house straightened up and the counters cleared and tidy.

Later, Kris called Patti and complained, "He just didn't get it. He didn't tell me how to love him; he only wanted me to keep the house cleaner."

"Maybe service is his love language," Patti replied.

"Oh, I never thought of that."

So Kris began to serve Dean, doing little things to keep their place tidy and neat. Later she called Patti. "This really works! I can't believe how much better he is treating me just because I'm doing a few little things to please him."

Time

As a love language, *time* does not mean two bodies in the same room or the same car. It means intimate talk and mutually enjoyed activities. It does not mean watching TV together, unless both partners want to, but rather active listening to one another. The emphasis is not on what is said—that is the love language of words. With time, the emphasis is on quality and quantity: what we say or do and how much of ourselves we put into it.

By the way, the time crunch is especially severe in the 30- and 40-age groups. Careers are demanding and the children are time-consuming. During these years, setting aside periods for tender talk or fun as a couple requires time management skills—the same discipline of time and energy usage that goes into our careers and children. It must have the same priority as eating or sleeping. We make time for what is most important to us. When the time simply is not currently available, it may mean making an appointment:

- "I can't talk right now, but I'll be free in just a few minutes."
- "Could we compare date books and find the best time for both of us?"
- "How about turning off the TV as soon as this program is over so we can talk?"
- "Have you thought about a weekly (or even monthly) date night?"
- "Let's go out for dinner and then do something we both enjoy."
- "Can you meet me for lunch?"
- "Let's make phone contact a couple times each day!"

Husbands and wives do not always share the same dialect when the love language is time, nor do they always understand each other when they simply try to communicate. As we mentioned, when men feel stressed, they often need to go into their caves to be alone for a while or, at the very least, to be silent. Men feel they lose something of themselves if they are always with their wives. When men are hurting, they honor each other by giving one another space. They seldom intrude into another man's private world unless they are asked or given specific permission. When men do talk, they usually express information or find solutions to problems.[6]

When women feel stressed, they often need to be with someone supportive and explore their feelings by talking. Women feel as if they lose something of themselves if they are seldom engaged in sharing real feelings. When women are hurting, they honor each other by giving one another support. They seldom withdraw their caring conversation unless the other person makes them feel unwanted or unwelcome. When women talk, they not only express information but also explore feelings and thoughts, create intimacy or simply try to feel better.[7]

Many men and women may share the same love language of time yet speak different dialects. When time is a man's love language, he may desire shared activity. He may want to go places, have fun, enjoy recreation and do the things they did together when they were dating. When a woman's love language is time, she may desire quiet time alone with her husband so they can enjoy intimate conversation. She may want to go out to dinner where they can talk uninterrupted, have some relaxed adult conversation (especially if she spends the day with toddlers and young children) and enjoy the kind of in-depth communication they had while they were dating. Each desires time, but with an entirely different focus: He focuses on doing; she focuses on feeling. (These gender stereotypes are occasionally reversed.)

Touch

During times of crisis or emotional trauma, people naturally tend to put their arms around one another. They sense the love that comes from a hug. Listen up, men: If your wife's love language is touch, always hold her close when she cries. (The only exception is when you made her cry and *she doesn't want you to touch her.*)

If a tragedy or crisis has occurred, hold each other as long as the tears flow. In times of intense pain, we need more of our primary love languages than ever before. This is the time to give love in the other person's language, even while we crave it in our own.

With touch, as in all of the love languages, understanding our spouse's preferences is vital. Some kinds of touching feel wonderful, while others are irritating. Hugs and kisses, holding hands and sitting close are strictly private acts for some, but more public for others. Using honesty and openness, we can learn the kinds of touching our partners enjoy most and the circumstances in which they are preferred.

Many men and some women, both Christian and non-Christian, judge the happiness of their marriages by the frequency of intercourse. Those with another primary love language may find the romance and passion involved more satisfying than the physical act itself. The Bible clearly directs husbands and wives to submit to one another's sexual needs (see 1 Cor. 7:3-6). However, meeting God-given sexual needs is not the same as trying to satisfy another's lust.

Our sex-saturated society with its pornography and deviant sexual behaviors causes many spouses to feel harassed and demeaned. Husbands are most likely to make unreasonable demands for weird sex. Usually, their wives resent it and wonder whether the Bible demands that they submit to what has been learned through pornography. (It doesn't, and wives shouldn't!) This is not a love language; it is a lust language. This is not spiritual obligation; it is spiritual abuse. Sexual harassment, abuse, addictions and other bondages can be broken through Christ, and freedom is so refreshing.[8]

Spouses should aggressively meet each other's sexual needs with the variety and passion described in the Song of Solomon. Sexual intercourse freely given may fill the love bank. However, spouses who give it grudgingly may actually cause the other person emotional pain.

Words

Do you recall this little ditty from grade school days?

Sticks and stones may break my bones,
but words will never hurt me.

We chanted it defiantly to protect ourselves from the mean and nasty remarks other kids said to us. In childhood innocence, we even may have believed it, but it was a lie.

Words hurt or heal. They criticize or compliment. They can be used to express harshness or kindness or to speak truth or lies. Words *do matter*, especially when spoken by someone we love, someone in our families, or someone close to us. Personal words touch our souls with extraordinary power.

Recently I (Chuck) wrote each of my grown children a love letter. I didn't call it that, of course. My message was tucked away in a paragraph or two among other more mundane matters. But the crucial paragraphs told them how much I loved them and why. Their mom, my wonderful wife, Nancy, added a simple note saying, "Ditto to everything Dad said" and "I couldn't agree more."

Their responses were heartening. Not only did these young adults appreciate their letters, but also my seemingly inadequate words empowered them with fresh strength. My words appeared to give them confidence in their relationships with Christ, in their characters and in their abilities. The effect of a few loving words can be amazing!

The same principle works in marriage. A woman whose husband had recently died of cancer spoke at the 1994 Promise Keepers Conference at Anaheim Stadium in California. She told how her thoughtful man had brought her a cup of coffee each morning along with a note. He simply drew a little Valentine saying why or how he loved her that day. This grief-stricken wife was a radiant witness to thousands of men about the power of a husband who gave away loving words. Both husbands and wives need to hear "I love you" every day, again and again. Combined with specific compliments about character, ability and intimacy, the words build up the marriage.

By the same token, destructive words tear down all relationships, including marriages and families. Often, the tone of our voices stirs up more trouble than the words we have spoken. Harshness, nagging, criticism, nit-picking and ridiculing—all these and more eat away at the souls of our marriages. Bridling our tongues requires God's grace and our utmost discipline, but it pays wonderful dividends. "A word out of your mouth may seem of no account, but it can accomplish nearly anything—or destroy it!" (Jas. 3:5, *THE MESSAGE*).

Why not use the blue stone method to discuss what both of you might feel comfortable doing or trying? A marriage counselor once taught this technique to his clients to help them talk through a touchy subject from their past without getting into an argument. The couple purchased a blue agate stone that was to be held by the person talking. The other had to remain quiet, except to summarize what the first person said. No distractions, interruptions or added comments were allowed unless the one who held the stone gave permission.

When the first person agreed that the second understood exactly what had been communicated, the stone was passed. Then the second person could respond, seeking the same understanding before giving up the stone. Or the one with the stone could bring up a new subject, explore another feeling or try to explain his or her own viewpoint. Whoever held the blue stone was in charge of the conversation until understanding was reached.

Passing the stone back and forth stopped interruptions, accusations and stomping out in anger. It was an old technique with a new twist. The stone became the ultimate arbiter of whose turn it was to control the conversation. Because the spouses agreed to work according to the rules, the blue stone guaranteed effective communication.

Our friend Bob Ramsey is a gifted thinker and writer. Listen to his colorful account and insightful wisdom about how essential it is to say the right thing at the right time:

Yogi Berra was one of the greatest baseball players of all time. He hit for power, and for average. He fielded his position without equal. Forty years after his prime, he continues to hold many of the hitting records for the World Series, and he was easily elected to the Hall of Fame.

Yogi is even more famous, however, for his grasp of the obvious, and for his personal twist on the English language. Fans and non-fans alike often collect what some call "Berra-isms," Yogi's unique perspectives on life and baseball. He was the first one to say, "It ain't over 'til it's over." When asked about his technique, he said, "90 percent of hitting is mental. The other half is physical." He once gave up going to a popular restaurant. His reason? "No one goes there anymore. It's too crowded."

Yogi's sayings were so famous, some believed they were being made up by witty sports writers with too much time on their hands. When asked about this, Yogi said, "I never said half the things I said."

"I never said half the things I said." How many of us wish we could say the same thing. We all have a backlog of things we wish we hadn't said. Maybe it was the tone of voice. Perhaps it was accidental, and you were mortified to find out the effect of what you had said. Maybe you even meant to be hurtful or spiteful, and only thought better of it later.

If I could be granted a super or magical power, I would want the ability to recall ill considered words. Perhaps even better though, would be the ability to say just the right words. I have seen the right words heal a long standing hurt. I have seen the wrong words almost destroy a person in just a few seconds.

The Bible tells us, in Proverbs 25:11, "A word aptly spoken is like apples of gold in settings of silver." The right word at the right time is a gift beyond any monetary value. It has a beauty which exceeds the finest craftsmanship.

Not many of us have the ability to create beauty with gold or silver. But the Lord is at work making us into masters of creating beauty and empowering others with our words. Let's give ourselves to learning this skill. And don't tell yourself it's too late to start or too hard to change. Remember, as Yogi said, "It ain't over 'til it's over."[9]

Why not ask your marriage partner, the members of your family and your close friends what their emotional love languages are—gifts, service, time, touch, words? Then try giving yourself away. You'll love it, and so will they!

Notes

1. Gary Chapman, *The Five Love Languages, How to Express Heartfelt Commitment to Your Mate* (Chicago: Northfield Publishing, 1992), p. 14.
2. Ibid., p. 76.
3. Rich Buhler, *LOVE: No Strings Attached* (Nashville, TN: Thomas Nelson Publishers, 1987), pp. 60-63.
4. Ibid., pp. 58-60.
5. Chapman, *The Five Love Languages*, pp. 89-96.
6. John Gray, *Men Are from Mars, Women Are from Venus, A Practical Guide for Improving Communication and Getting What You Want in Your Relationships* (New York: Harper Collins Publishers, 1988), pp. 59-91.
7. Ibid.
8. We have each written on this subject earlier. See Neil T. Anderson, *Finding Freedom in a Sex-Obsessed World* (Eugene, OR: Harvest House Publishers, 2003); and Charles Mylander, *Running the Red Lights, Putting the Brakes on Sexual Temptation* (Ventura, CA: Regal Books, 1986).
9. Bob Ramsey, "Apt Words," *The Encourager, News and Views from the Headquarters of the Friends Church Southwest Yearly Meeting*, December 9, 1994, pp. 1-2.

Group Discussion

1. What is your primary love language? What is your spouse's love language?

2. Can you think of a time when not understanding each other's love language caused you some pain?

3. What was one time when you felt most loved and appreciated?

4. If you had the time, how would you like to spend it with your spouse?

5. Can you think of a time when you thought you were doing the loving thing for your spouse, but your efforts weren't appreciated? How did you feel?

Devotional Guide for Couples

Read James 3:13-18 and then share your love language with each other and explain how your spouse can best love you with it.

THE ROOT OF ALL EVIL

*You can't worship two gods at once. Loving one god, you'll end up hating the other.
Adoration of one feeds contempt for the other. You can't worship God and Money both.*

*If you decide for God, living a life of God-worship, it follows that you don't fuss about
what's on the table at mealtimes or whether the clothes in your closet are in fashion.*

*Instead of looking at the fashions, walk out into the fields and look at the wildflowers.
They never primp or shop, but have you ever seen color and design quite like it?
The ten best-dressed men and women in the country look shabby alongside them.*

*If God gives such attention to the appearance of wildflowers—most of which are never
even seen—don't you think he'll attend to you, take pride in you, do his best for you?
What I'm trying to do here is to get you to relax, to not be so preoccupied with getting,
so you can respond to God's giving. People who don't know God and the way he works
fuss over these things, but you know both God and how he works. Steep your life in
God-reality, God-initiative, God-provisions. Don't worry about missing out.
You'll find all your everyday human concerns will be met.*

MATTHEW 6:24-25,28-33, *THE MESSAGE*

Once upon a time, there lived a peanut vendor in South India. Every day he walked up and down the beach calling out, "Peanuts! Peanuts for sale! Peanuts!" The man was miserably poor. He barely earned half a living, hardly enough to feed his family. But at night he bragged to his wife and children, "I am the president, vice president, secretary and treasurer of my own company!"

The grinding poverty wore his nerves paper thin. One day, he snapped. He sold all his peanuts and most of his meager belongings. He decided to go on a big fling. "For one day I am going to live like a rich man!" he vowed. So he stopped by the barber for a shave and a trim. He visited a fine men's clothing store and purchased an expensive suit, white shirt and tie, and all the accessories needed to look rich. Then he checked himself into the finest luxury hotel for the night. He had just enough money left to pay for the gourmet breakfast buffet the next morning.

He enjoyed the night's accommodations in his luxury suite. When morning came, he located the private, beachfront patio for the breakfast buffet. Although it was crowded with tourists, he found a table by himself. He had just filled his plate when in walked a man who was elegantly dressed. By this time, no more tables were available, so the man moved toward him and asked, "May I join you?"

The peanut vendor replied, "Why, yes! Please sit down." He was thinking to himself, "This is my lucky day! Not only am I living like a rich man, I am also going to eat with a rich man."

As the two began to talk, the stranger asked, "What do you do?"

"I am the president, vice president, secretary and treasurer of my own company," he replied. "And what do you do?"

The richly dressed man looked a bit sheepish. "I'm sorry. I should have introduced myself. I just supposed that with the coverage in the newspapers you might have recognized me. My name is John D. Rockefeller."

Although he had not recognized the face, the peanut vendor did know the name. He thought to himself, "This is wonderful! I am eating with one of the richest men in the whole world."

After talking for a while, Mr. Rockefeller said, "I like your style. We are starting a new company here in South India. Why don't you come to work for me? I will make you vice president of sales in my new firm."

The peanut vendor replied, "Why, thank you. What a generous offer! I would like a few minutes to think it over."

"Of course," said Mr. Rockefeller, "but I would like some indication of your interest before we part company."

The two leisurely enjoyed the rest of their meal. When they were finished, the peanut vendor stood up. He wanted to announce his decision with style. He took a step away from the table, and then turned and spoke in a voice loud enough that many could overhear, "Thank you, Mr. Rockefeller, for offering me the position of vice president in your new company. But I must decline. I prefer to be the president, vice president, secretary and treasurer of my own company." He turned on his heel and walked out.

Years later, an old peanut vendor walked up and down the same resort beaches croaking in a broken voice, "Peanuts! Peanuts for sale! Peanuts!" But at night, he boasted to his grandchildren that long ago one of the richest men in the world offered to make him vice president of a huge firm.

"I turned it down," he bragged, "so that I could be the president, vice president, secretary and treasurer of my own company."[1]

A foolish man, but we are in effect doing the same thing when we don't commit all our finances to God. We are turning down a partnership with the Lord of unlimited riches. We want to be the president and the vice president and the secretary and the treasurer of our own enterprise. In light of eternity, we keep working for what amounts to peanuts!

Finding Security

Annual income greater than annual expenses equals a tranquil marriage. Annual expenses greater than annual income equals a marriage in pain. Money and marriage are interrelated, but they do not always mix well. Deep within the human psyche is an inner longing for security. We want to know we will be safe and cared for. We desire protection from anything that threatens our cherished way of life.

What makes us feel secure? Money? House? Family? Circumstances under control? Law and order? In varying degrees, these may increase our temporal feelings of security, yet in our heart we know that tangible and outward things are not enough to supply the eternal security we all long for. The bombing of the Trade Centers revealed our vulnerability. The collapse of Enron revealed the corporate greed that is rampant throughout the industry. At the end of the day, nothing in this world provides lasting security. Consider the following:

- Money can vanish quickly. Bankruptcies, lawsuits and late payments are commonplace.
- Houses can be foreclosed or forced into sale. The number of homeless is on the increase.
- Families can be fractured by divorce due to financial mismanagement.
- Natural disasters, such as the hurricane that destroyed New Orleans as well as the Mississippi and Florida coastal communities, can cause death, displacement and relocation.
- Law enforcement cannot stop crime. Child and spousal abuse, thefts, murders, rapes and other crimes continue to take their toll.

Yet there is hope for each of us: Since God puts the longing for security in our hearts, He intends to fulfill it. He is our Rock, a favorite Old Testament name that suggests protection, stability and security:

May the words of my mouth and the meditation of my heart be pleasing in your sight, O LORD, *my Rock* and my Redeemer (Ps. 19:14, emphasis added).

Whenever the Bible uses the term "my rock" for God, we can accurately substitute "my security." Eternal security can only be found in our relationship with God. He is always there, always reliable, always the same. Through the cross and the Resurrection, He provides eternal life that transcends death, character that triumphs over tragedy, and peace that wins over anxiety. In Christ, our security is as solid as a rock (see Rom. 8:35-39).

The apostle Paul taught that contentment was far better than loving money and seeking riches (see 1 Tim. 6:3-10). James warned those who think they are rich that misery may be coming on them (see Jas. 5:1). Jesus taught that financial security was not something to worry about, for real security was found by seeking first God's kingdom (see Matt. 6:25-34).

Where You Have Say

A kingdom has a ruler, a realm and a reign. The kingdom of heaven is God's rule, God's reign, God's government. The Church is God's realm, and He rules in those hearts that are fully yielded to Him. The kingdom of God is embodied in Jesus Christ. He is King (Lord), and everything in heaven and on Earth is under His ultimate authority (see Eph. 1:20-23). Even while He was on Earth in a physical body, the love and power of the Kingdom flowed through Him. He had more influence and more say than anyone else who ever lived.

Dallas Willard, professor of philosophy at the University of Southern California, described the Kingdom as the effective range of God's will. In other words, what is under God's daily control and what conforms to His will is in His kingdom. What is not, in actual practice, under God's control and fails to do His will is not in His kingdom.

We like to sit on the throne of our own kingdoms. Our kingdom is where we have our say: how fast we drive, what we eat, the money we spend—all according to what we say. Our kingdom includes what is under our own control, what we have the ability to decide. Our kingdom is where we assume the right to choose. One of the benefits—as well as dangers—of becoming an adult is that we have more say: We have more choices to determine our destinies and more money to express our values. In short, we have larger kingdoms, but they cannot last.

What Jesus desires is for us to build His kingdom and not ours. He wants us to bring our marriages and our daily lives, including our finances, into God's kingdom. We first become children of God, subjects of the Kingdom, by accepting Jesus Christ as Lord and Savior—as our King! Yet it is possible, even likely, that not all of our financial habits are in His kingdom, not all of our own rule is under His rule, and not all of our personal say is under His say (see Matt. 6:10,33).

Two parts of my (Chuck) own kingdom—two places where I have say—came to my attention recently. One was my cluttered desk, and the other was how I drive. (By the way, both of these bad habits have caused my wife to feel insecure.) If these are to become part of God's kingdom in my daily life, I must change. I must exercise simple obedience to what I already know is God's will. So I have started bringing the effective range of my will under the effective range of God's will. For me, this includes putting things away, rather than letting my desk become cluttered, and driving more safely.

I let my desk get messy because I am lazy, because I make some wrong choices, or because I become too busy. I let my driving get lousy because I'm preoccupied, because I'm in a hurry, or because I leave too late. It is easy to think I will change, but I meet resistance. Laziness, poor choices, busyness, preoccupied thoughts and a habit of hurrying do not change easily. I will have to go into training and keep practicing. It will take a trainload of God's grace *and* a carload of my discipline to pull these bad traits into God's kingdom.

Other parts of our life—attitudes, motives, desires—also need to be aligned with God's will. What does it take to love more, to worship more genuinely and to think more clearly? What about our marriage, family and finances? Will we invite Christ to put us together, set us right, complete us with joy? Submitting ourselves to the kingdom of God requires more than trying harder; it requires the power of God. We need to surrender our reign and crown to Him, our King. Submission takes all the resources and riches Christ provides. It takes a heart relationship that wants to please Him.

Money is the king in many struggling marriages in which the rationalizations and complaints sound something like this:

- "The kingdom of God is fine for church, but *my money* is something I prefer to control."
- "It's in style. Of course I need it."
- "I really wanted a nicer car."
- "I'm working all these hours so you can be well taken care of, sweetheart. It's all for you."
- "If only you didn't spend so much on yourself . . ."
- "If only you made more money . . ."

Craving Money

Take a few moments to make a fearless moral inventory. Go through the following Scriptures and ask yourself, *Whom do I really serve between*

Sundays? Is it the God who revealed Himself in Jesus Christ, or is it money? Does my money help me serve God, or do I expect God to help me make more money?

- Paul states, "The love of money is a root of all kinds of evil. Some people, eager for money, have wandered from the faith and pierced themselves with many griefs" (1 Tim. 6:10).
- One of the requirements for overseers and elders is that they not be "lover[s] of money" (1 Tim. 3:3).
- Christians are commanded to put to death whatever belongs to their earthly nature, including "greed, which is idolatry" (Col. 3:5).
- Jesus taught, "You cannot serve both God and Money" (Matt. 6:24).
- The Bible specifically warns against a desire to get rich: "People who want to get rich fall into temptation and a trap and into many foolish and harmful desires that plunge men into ruin and destruction" (1 Tim. 6:9).

Serving God gives both present and eternal rewards. Serving money leads to a decaying character and a dying society. The following parable describes the relationship between God, us and our money.

The Ten Apples

Once upon a time, God gave a prehistoric man 10 red apples. None of the people who lived near him had tasted apples before. They would give almost anything for an apple.

God told the man to trade three of the apples for a cave. It would shelter his family from the wind and rain. The man obeyed God and found a good cave. For three apples, the owner sold him the cave.

God told the man to trade three of the apples for clothing. It would cover his family's bodies and warm them during wet, chilly weather. The man obeyed God and found a trader with skin garments. He traded three apples for clothes for his whole family.

God told the man to trade three of the apples for food to eat. It would sustain and nourish his family. The man obeyed God and traded one apple each for fruit, grain and meat.

Then God told the man to give one apple back to Himself as a gift. It would serve as a symbol of thanksgiving, relation-ship and love. It would allow God to plant the last apple and produce many more apples in the years to come. The man had already traded three apples for a cave, three for clothes and three for food. He had only one apple left.

The man looked at his last apple. It looked bigger and shinier than any of the others. He could imagine its sweet taste. He could smell its sweet aroma as he held it near his mouth. He longed to sink his teeth into the delicious apple, to savor its juices.

The man reasoned that God could create an apple tree if He wanted to. God really didn't need this one last apple to plant as a blessing for his future. So he ate the last apple—and gave back to God the core!

Some people consume the money God trusts into their care. They spend most of it on necessities, some on little pleasures, and then give God the leftovers. Tragedy of tragedies, they miss the blessings God promised.

"Greed," "avarice," "cupidity"—these words used to describe lusting after money are not often part of our daily conversations. Instead, we admire the rich and pity the poor. The bitter truth is that lust for money brings trouble into our marriages and families. The problem with grabbing for whatever attracts our fancy is that it bypasses the will of God. A lust for money is shaped by feelings and things, not by our

Lord Jesus. Eugene Peterson's paraphrase of Colossians 3:5-6 warns us of how our cravings for money make God feel: "It's because of this kind of thing that God is about to explode in anger" (*THE MESSAGE*).

Why is God so angry?

- Because our lust for money replaces our love for God.
- Because it twists and warps our God-given desire to help the poor.
- Because it cripples our efforts to support His churches and ministries.

So what is a believer to do in this materialistic society?

- Admit that God is the owner of everything, including our money.
- Learn contentment, the kind that comes with godliness.
- Find delight in simple pleasures.
- Become a wise steward of all the resources God gives, including our finances.
- Give more, live on less.

Money has a good side and a bad side. Its good side is what it provides—daily needs for our family, support for ministry, even a few enjoyable luxuries in life. Its bad side is what loving money destroys—compassion, self-sacrifice and intense love for God.

The love of money, and what money can buy, creates havoc in many marriages. No surprise. We each want what we want and find ways to buy it. Then the bills and monthly payments stack up until there is no more credit. When a genuine emergency occurs—medical expenses, car breakdown, job loss—we're overwhelmed. Tensions rise as we each blame the other for spending too much or not earning enough. All too often, these financial pressures contribute to divorce.

The good side of money becomes the bad side. What provided for our needs and pleasures has now turned into payments due and no way to pay. Resolving the conflict between husband and wife may bring temporary relief, but a lasting solution will not come until we submit our love for money to Christ and bring our earning and spending into the kingdom of God.

We do not change our financial habits permanently without changing who we are on the inside. Believing God's truth precedes living Christ's way. To put it simply, we must believe God's truth about money before we will change our spending habits. We must honor God with our finances before we can expect Him to honor us with inner contentment.

God Owns Everything

The biggest difference between God's economy and man's economy is *stewardship* and *ownership*. In man's economy, people own things. In God's economy, God owns everything. He entrusts it to us, and we are to be good stewards (see 1 Cor. 4:1). He created the heavens and the earth and all that is in it (see Gen. 1:1; Ps. 146:6; Isa. 44:24; Col. 1:15-17; Rev. 4:11) and He retains ownership of everything He created. Meditate on the following Scriptures:

> To the LORD your God belong the heavens, even the highest heavens, the earth *and everything in it* (Deut. 10:14, emphasis added).

> Yours, O LORD, is the greatness and the power and the glory and the majesty and the splendor, *for everything in heaven and earth is yours.* Yours, O LORD, is the kingdom; you are exalted as head over all (1 Chron. 29:11, emphasis added).

> *The earth is the LORD's and everything in it,* the world, and all who live in it (Ps. 24:1, emphasis added).

For every animal of the forest is mine, and the cattle on a thousand hills. I know every bird in the mountains, and the creatures of the field are mine. If I were hungry I would not tell you, *for the world is mine, and all that is in it* (Ps. 50:10-12, emphasis added).

God owns everything! Our culture teaches that God has nothing to do with money, except the use of "charitable giving." Everything else belongs to us—and the government! Because of the pressure of this world's system, we need to remind ourselves again and again that all money and material things in our care belong to God and that we should:

- Pursue good management of the Lord's money and resources
- Consult the Lord and seek wise counsel in financial decisions
- Pray more often, "Give us today our daily bread"
- Rejoice in knowing that God provides and blesses
- Learn contentment when God withdraws our financial resources to teach us to trust Him
- Actually act like God is in charge of our money!

Generous People

As he walked out of church, a young boy asked the pastor, "What are you going to do with my dad's quarter?" His father hadn't tithed; he had tipped. Some people are like this young boy's dad: They don't tithe; they tip. They disobey God and suffer the consequences. Worse yet, they miss the seed of generosity that God wanted to plant in their hearts. Generous people are blessed:

Generous people are fun to be around.
    They have so many friends.
Generous people can be trusted.
    They are givers, not takers.

Generous people are kind.

They reach out to the poor and needy.

Generous people get outside of themselves.

They care about the lost.

Generous people never go hungry.

They find that God and their friends rush to their aid.

In my youth, I heard an old saint say, "Never deny a generous impulse." That simple thought has stuck with me for years. Now I know why: "God loves a cheerful giver" (2 Cor. 9:7). Throughout the Bible, tithing is used as the standard guide for giving. Tithing means a tenth goes to God, right off the top. God commanded it in the Old Testament and commended it in the New Testament (see Lev. 27:30-32; Mal. 3:10; Matt. 23:23). God doesn't bless what we keep. He blesses what we sow in His kingdom.

You get out of life what you put into it. If you want a friend, be a friend. If you want someone to love you, love someone. The more you give, the more you receive. Don't just try it. Make it a life commitment, and you will be blessed.

The Joy of Contentment

The financial goal in marriage is not to become rich but to become content in Christ. Contentment comes from security in Christ and healthy relationships as well as from being a good financial steward. (Note that six of the seven references to contentment in the New Testament are in a context of money.) Paul wrote:

Not that I speak from want, for I have learned to be content in whatever circumstances I am. I know how to get along with humble means, and I also know how to live in prosperity; in any and every circumstance I have learned the secret of being filled and going hungry, both of having abundance and suffering need (Phil. 4:11-12, *NASB*).

Contentment is part of our sanctifying process, yet few of us find that contentment comes easily or stays long. The following suggestions may help.

Sign It All Over to God
One of Satan's lies is that we own our money and property rather than serve as God's trustees of material things. One way to rivet God's ownership in our minds is to make up a quitclaim deed, signing over to God all the possessions the Lord has given us.[2] Consider changing your vocabulary from "my" to "the." Talk about "the" car and "the" house instead of "my" car and "my" house. This is a small discipline to remind ourselves that everything we have belongs to God, not us.

Practice Gratitude
Few things build contentment like thanking God. Praising God for everything He has given us changes greed to gratitude. Christians are the richest people on Earth! We have everything money can't buy and thieves can't steal. We are rich in God and have treasures in heaven! In the here and now, we have all of God's resources and riches, plus many material benefits He showers on us. What's more, God takes care of His children financially. King David sang:

> I was young and now I am old, yet I have never seen the righteous forsaken or their children begging bread. They are always generous and lend freely; their children will be blessed (Ps. 37:25-26).

I have noticed over the years that missionaries who work for a mere pittance in foreign countries have children who seem to prosper financially.

A high percentage of their children graduate from private Christian colleges in spite of the high costs. God provides when we respond to how He guides. He gives us everything we need for doing His will—and bonuses as well. One of His incredible promises relates to eternal prosperity: "And everyone who has left houses or brothers or sisters or father or mother or children or fields for my sake will receive a hundred times as much and will inherit eternal life" (Matt. 19:29). No wonder we are grateful!

Resolve Differences

In marriage, how we spend our money reflects our values. The husband wants to spend the money one way and the wife another. Of course! We are different people with differing values, desires and tastes. Even our view of what's an absolute need and what is a mere want differs drastically. The sooner a married couple agrees on basic principles and values for using their money, the better. This is why the process of budgeting may be as useful as the budget itself. Budgets establish priorities.

Conflict about money, even about being a good steward of it, cannot be avoided in marriage. So we should face the conflict, work it through, get the problem resolved, and then work out minor differences as they arise. Couples who fight about money experience trouble and seldom resolve their problems. They keep up their bad habits and blame each other for the mess they're in.

It may help to think in percentages. What percentage will we give to the Lord's work? What percentage will we save? The old adage "Give 10 percent, save 10 percent, and spend the rest with joy," isn't bad for starters! But stay alert to the Holy Spirit's guidance.

Manage Finances Wisely

Nowhere in the Bible are we commanded to make a budget. However, a major theme of God's Word is the fact that we are accountable for how we use money. One of the shockers in Jesus' teaching was that the way we handle money serves as the training ground for handling spiritual riches. Our Lord taught, "So if you have not been trustworthy in handling worldly wealth, who will trust you with true riches?" (Luke 16:11). A budget proves useful because it forces us to plan our giving and monitor our use of money. Financial crisis counselors report no incoming clients who regularly use a budget.

Reduce Debt

The biggest trap for most consumers today is debt. Credit card companies, finance companies and banks are getting rich from interest! Advertisers perfect the art of increasing our desires and decreasing our satisfaction. Then they dupe us into thinking in terms of monthly payments instead of total price. Before long the issue becomes, "Can we afford the payment?" rather than, "Do we have the cash to buy it?" The Bible says that debt is *slavery:*

> The rich rule over the poor,
> And the borrower is servant to the lender (Prov. 22:7).

If you don't believe this proverb, try skipping two or three car payments and see what happens! Debt is bondage. Worse yet, the Bible teaches that debt is one of the curses God sends if we disobey Him (see Deut. 28:15,43-44). Debt is a curse. Why would anyone want to live under slavery, bondage and a curse? Howard L. Dayton suggests 10 commonsense guidelines for escaping this bondage:

1. Pray.
2. Establish a written budget.
3. List your assets—everything you own.

4. List your liabilities—everything you owe.

5. Establish a debt repayment schedule for each creditor.

6. Consider earning additional income.

7. Accumulate no new debt.

8. Be content with what you have.

9. Consider a radical lifestyle change.

10. Do not give up![3]

Give Generously

If debt is a curse, giving is a blessing. Love is the heart of giving. We are not to give reluctantly as we muse, *Just think what I could do with all this money.* Nor are we to give under compulsion as we think, *Rats! To be a good Christian, I have to tithe.* Remember, it all belongs to God.

The good news is that givers prosper. Other people know that givers are generous, honest and kind, so they like to do business with them. In addition, God always keeps His promises, including the ones about rewarding us in proportion to our generosity (see Luke 6:38; 2 Cor. 9:6-8,11). When we give our money to Christ's work, our hearts follow our treasures (see Luke 12:32-34). Note three practical principles from God's Word regarding how we ought to be generous:

1. Give before we can afford it (see 2 Cor. 8:2)

2. Give beyond our ability (see v. 3)

3. Give first to the Lord (see v. 5)

Invest Wisely

Saving consistently prepares for future difficulties—and those troubles are sure to come (see Prov. 21:20). Worthy goals for saving and investing are to provide for our family, operate a business, or free up our time to serve God. Unworthy goals include a desire to get rich and to build a false sense of security in wealth (see Luke 12:13-21; 1 Tim. 6:9).

Diligent planning leads to a profit, but rushing into an investment leads to loss (see Prov. 21:5). In business, in investments and in life, constant alertness is necessary (see Prov. 27:23-24). Wise investors do not put all their eggs in one basket; they diversify (see Eccles. 11:1-2).

Financial Ethics

In a culture such as ours that is devoted to greed and built on the false god of money, every Christian and every godly family needs a code of financial ethics. Although much could be added to what follows, not much can be subtracted, for these 12 principles are based on God's written Word:

1. We will avoid greed and be honest in all our financial dealings. We will not lie, cheat, steal or beat people out of money (see Deut. 5:19-21; 25:15-16; Prov. 20:10,23; Luke 12:15; Eph. 4:28).

2. We will show God's love with the money He entrusts to us. We will put God first in our lives through giving tithes and offerings. We will give to the church, to missions, to the poor and especially to the needy among our own families, relatives and Christian friends (see Deut. 14:22-23; 1 Chron. 29:11-14; Mal. 3:8-10; Matt. 23:23-25; Luke 6:38; 11:42; Acts 20:35; Rom. 13:9-10; 1 Tim. 5:8; 6:18-19).

3. We will pay our debts promptly and seek to stay out of debt (see Ps. 37:21; Prov. 3:27-28; 22:7; Matt. 5:25-26; Rom. 13:8). We will not co-sign for another's debts (Prov. 6:1-5; 17:18; 22:26-27).

4. We will save a portion of our incomes for future difficulties (see Prov. 13:11; 21:20; 30:24-25; note the cautions about oversaving taught by Jesus in Matt. 6:19-20,24-26; Luke 12:16-21).

5. We will avoid risky investments and get-rich-quick schemes (see Prov. 28:20-22; Eccles. 5:13-15; 1 Tim. 6:9-10).

6. We will look for investments that produce redemptive results, not destructive ones. We will use our investment money for God's glory (see Lev. 25:47-55; Ps. 49:20; 1 Cor. 10:31; Col. 3:17; 1 Tim. 6:17-19).

7. We will live by the highest standards of financial integrity in our families, our churches, and our chosen work or professions (see Job 1:8; Ps. 112:1-10; Prov. 10:2; 11:3,18; Matt. 7:12; 2 Cor. 7:2).

8. We will neither oppress the poor nor bribe the rich (see Exod. 23:8; Prov. 15:27; 22:16,22-23; Isa. 5:22-23; 33:15).

9. We will make restitution for any wrongs we have committed against the person or property of another (see Lev. 6:1-5; Num. 5:5-7; Prov. 6:30-31; Ezek. 33:14,15; Luke 19:8-10).

10. We will not use the courts for lawsuits against other believers or engage in any unethical legal proceedings designed to gain unjust money (see Exod. 23:1-3; Lev. 19:15; 25:17; Deut. 1:17; 2 Chron. 19:5-7; Prov. 24:23; Zech. 8:16-17; Luke 12:13-15; 1 Cor. 6:1-8).

11. We will work faithfully and diligently for our incomes as good stewards of the Lord (see Prov. 12:11; 13:4; 1 Cor. 4:2; Eph. 6:5-9; Col. 3:23,24; 4:1; 1 Thess. 2:9; 2 Thess. 3:6-13).

12. We will balance work and rest (see Exod. 20:8-11; Deut. 5:12-15; Ps. 127:1-2; Heb. 4:1-11).

Money and marriage can mix well if both are centered in God. Time and discipline are needed to master our money for God's glory, to bring it fully into His kingdom. When King Jesus rules both our marriage and our money (what a glorious thought!), we receive the rewards. Then we experience the benefits of the Kingdom—righteousness, peace and joy in the Holy Spirit. We become pleasing to God and respected by the people who matter most to us (see Rom. 14:17-18). The kingdom of God is good news—great news! It brings God's best—forgiveness, cleansing, gifts, fruit of the Spirit, character, virtue, joy, light, life—and much more! Happy marriages, good families, satisfying careers and healthy finances are often the byproducts.

Money, used wisely for God's glory, helps build a happy marriage. Money misused foolishly for personal gain helps create an unhappy marriage.

Notes

1. Dr. Mylander first heard the peanut vendor story from Dr. Sam Kameleson, Vice President of World Vision International, at the 1987 International Friends Conference on Evangelism in Guatemala City, Guatemala.
2. Crown Financial Ministries, an organization that provides excellent courses on Christian discipleship and finances, can provide a form you can use. For more information on this excellent Bible study, including *Small Group Financial Study* and *Practical Application Workbook*, write to: Crown Ministries, 530 Crown Oak Centre Drive, Longwood, FL 32750 or visit the organization on the web at www.crown.org.
3. Crown Ministries, *Small Group Financial Study* (Longwood, FL: Crown Ministries), pp. 40-43.

Group Discussion

1. What is the difference between stewardship and ownership? How can assuming you have ownership of your possessions affect your marriage and ministries?

2. How can a Christian be secure?

3. Why is it more blessed to give than to receive, and why doesn't every Christian believe this truth and live accordingly?

4. How can you learn to be more content?

5. Is it possible to live debt free in our present society? How?

Devotional Guide for Couples

Read 1 Timothy 6:6-12 and share with each other your own personal convictions concerning money, security and contentment.

SEXUAL FREEDOM

It is good for a man not to marry. But since there is so much immorality,
each man should have his own wife, and each woman her own husband.
The husband should fulfill his marital duty to his wife, and likewise the wife
to her husband. The wife's body does not belong to her alone but also to her
husband. In the same way, the husband's body does not belong to him alone
but also to his wife. Do not deprive each other except by mutual consent and
for a time, so that you may devote yourselves to prayer. Then come together
again so Satan will not tempt you because of your lack of self-control.

1 Corinthians 7:1-5

A few years ago I (Neil) conducted a "For Women Only" seminar. Because I was the only male there, I felt a little vulnerable. After lunch, the ladies suggested I would be more comfortable if I took off my coat. I said, "Okay, but that's all I'm taking off!" I told them I would honestly answer, to the best of my ability, any questions they asked. For those who didn't want to ask their questions in front of the others, they could write them out and leave them in a basket at the back of the room.

Did I get questions! Most of the written questions dealt with sex in marriage. If I could synthesize their questions into one, it would be, "Do I have to do whatever my husband wants me to do in bed?"

Biblical Guidelines

To answer that question, refer to the 1 Corinthians 7:1-5 passage quoted at the beginning of this chapter. It may be noble that one not marry in order to serve the Lord, but I'm sure it's not normal. Sexual immorality was obviously a problem in those days, just as it is today. This passage seems to be the sexual corollary to Ephesians 5:21: "Submit to one another out of reverence for Christ." Notice the spiritual dimension of the marital relationship. If we are not going to have sex with our spouses, it should be only because we have decided to abstain for the purpose of prayer for a mutually agreed upon time. We are not to withhold ourselves from our spouses, because that would give Satan an opportunity to take advantage of our lack of self-control. We should never use sex as a weapon or a means to get even.

Okay, I still haven't directly answered the question, "Do I have to do whatever my spouse wants?" I suspect the heart of this question is the husband's problem with lust. His rationalization might sound something like this: *The Bible says her body belongs to me. My wife should submit to whatever turns me on. It is her responsibility to meet my sexual needs.* Let's look at what the Bible says about this subject: "Marriage should be honored by all, and the marriage bed kept pure, for God will judge the adulterer and all the sexually immoral" (Heb. 13:4). So what does a wife (or husband) have to submit to?

First, a wife can and should meet the sexual needs of her husband, and vice versa. She is the only one who can do it without guilt or shame. But she cannot resolve his problem with lust. Men who struggle with lust somehow think their wives are responsible for resolving it. They falsely reason, *If my wife would only dress more sexy or participate in some kinky sex act, then I wouldn't have this problem.* That view is degrading. Even if she tried to be the sex object of his fantasy, it would only increase the lust. Lust is a sinful bondage that only Christ can break.

Second, we never have the right to violate another person's conscience (see Rom. 14). If our spouses believe a certain sexual act is wrong, then it is wrong for both of us. If we violate the other person's conscience, we destroy the trust in the relationship and undermine the vulnerability that is crucial to real sexual fulfillment. Time and tenderness will overcome the inhibitions. Scripture says, "What is desirable in a man is his kindness" (Prov. 19:22, *NASB*), not his crudeness. God created a helpmate for Adam, not a playmate.

I have asked the ladies in my conferences throughout the world, "If you had to choose between the character traits of strong masculinity or kindness in your husband, which would you choose?" Without hesitation, they all say, "Kindness."

My wife once asked me, "Do you know when you really turn me on?" I flexed my muscles a little and asked, "When?" She responded, "When you are kind to our children!"

Sexual Bondage

Sexual bondage destroys many marriages. The origin of the problem can usually be traced to pornography use, promiscuity, incest and rape that occurred *before* marriage. Getting married will not resolve sexual bondage. In fact, in many cases the problem just becomes exacerbated. I have dealt extensively with this problem of sexual bondage and freedom in my book *Finding Freedom in a Sex-Obsessed World* (Harvest House, 2003). In this chapter, I will highlight the essential issues, especially as they relate to marriage.

It would be great if we all had perfect parents who had taught us the truth about love and sex, but such is not the case. Many have been raised in pagan and/or broken homes, and many Christian homes are also dysfunctional. Consequently, our children are seldom afforded the opportunity to develop their sexuality as God intended. The effect can be felt in the succeeding generations. Let's examine King David's sexually dysfunctional family to understand the steps that led to his defilement and that of his sons.

"One evening David got up from his bed and walked around on the roof of the palace. From the roof he saw a woman bathing. The woman was very beautiful, and David sent someone to find out about her" (2 Sam. 11:2-3). Nothing is wrong with Bathsheba being beautiful, and nothing is wrong with David being attracted to her. God created us to be attracted to the opposite sex. Bathsheba may have been wrong for bathing where others could see her, and David was definitely wrong for continuing to look at her. God provided a way of escape, but David did not take it. Instead, he sent someone to find out about her. I wonder if this costly choice was the catalyst for God's inspiring Solomon (David's son) to write Proverbs 7:6-23:

At the window of my house I looked out through the lattice. I saw among the simple, I noticed among the young men, a youth who lacked judgment. He was going down the street near her corner, walking along in the direction of her house at twilight, as the day was fading, as the dark of night set in. Then out came a woman to meet him, dressed like a prostitute and with crafty intent. (She is loud and defiant, her feet never stay at home; now in the street, now in the squares, at every corner she lurks.) She took hold of him and kissed him and with a brazen face she said:

"I have fellowship offerings at home; today I fulfilled my vows. So I came out to meet you; I looked for you and have found you! I have covered my bed with colored linens from Egypt. I have perfumed my bed with myrrh, aloes and cinnamon. Come, let's drink deep of love till morning; let's enjoy ourselves with love! My husband is not at home; he has gone on a long journey. He took his purse filled with money and will not be home till full moon."

With persuasive words she led him astray; she seduced him with her smooth talk. All at once he followed her like an ox going to slaughter, like a deer stepping into a noose till an arrow pierces his liver, like a bird darting into a snare, little knowing it will cost him his life.

This married and seductive woman claimed to be religious. She prepared her home and then planned the event to be carried out under the cover of darkness. Such is the nature of sexual temptation. If we yield, our minds see only the immediate gratification of sexual desires, but never the consequences. The way of escape is only powerfully available the moment our minds register the first thoughts of temptation. Once we allow our minds to entertain thoughts contrary to God's Word, a whole chain of physiological responses is set in motion. The more we contemplate the sin, the more emotionally involved we become, and the less likely we will be to stand against it.

The Way of Escape

If we are going to take the way of escape God has provided for us, we must take the original thought captive to the obedience of Christ (see 2 Cor. 10:5). If we allow ourselves to dwell on tempting thoughts, we will eventually take paths that lead to destruction. For instance, suppose a man is struggling with lust. One night, his wife asks him to go to the store for some milk. When he gets in his car, he pauses to decide which store he should go to. He decides on a local convenience store. He knows the convenience store has a display of pornography. He does not have to go to that store. He could get the milk in a much safer environment, such as an all-night supermarket.

The battle for his mind has already been lost the moment he starts driving to the wrong store. Before he even leaves the garage, all kinds of compromising thoughts cross his mind. For instance, *If you don't want me to look at the pornography, Lord, have my pastor be at the store buying milk or cause a wreck in the intersection.* When there is no wreck and the pastor isn't there at the store, he reasons it must be okay to take a look.

The mind has an incredible propensity to rationalize, but the justifications don't last. Before the man has even left the store, guilt and shame overwhelm him. The tempter (Satan) switches strategies and becomes the accuser. The choice to take the way of escape had to be made before the man got into his car. Rare is the person who can turn the car around once the plan has been set in motion.

That is why the concept of "adults only" is fundamentally flawed—it implies there is a separate standard of morality for adults and for children. Adults should be mature enough to know that they should not allow their minds to be programmed with filth. Television programs come with the warning, "The content of the following movie is suitable for mature audiences only. Viewer discretion is advised." It isn't suitable for anyone, and mature people should be the first to know that. We have already been advised by God not to watch.

Often we choose to watch anyway, which is certainly what David did. When he sent messengers to get Bathsheba, he was too far down the trail of temptation to turn around. They slept together, and she became pregnant. Here comes the cover-up! David called for Uriah, her husband, to come home from the battlefield, but he wouldn't sleep with Bathsheba while his men on the field were being deprived. So David invited Uriah to stay another day and tried to get him drunk. He still wouldn't sleep with her. Then David sent orders for him to be strategically placed in battle so that he would be killed. Uriah died on the battlefield. Now David had become a murderer as well as an adulterer! Sin has a way of compounding itself. Living righteously is difficult, but living unrighteously is even more difficult. Cover-up, denial and guilt make for a very complex life.

After a period of mourning, David married Bathsheba. He lived with his guilt and covered his shame for nine months. The Lord allowed plenty of time for David to come to terms with his own sin. He didn't, so God sent him the prophet Nathan who told David a story about a rich man who ripped off the only lamb of a poor man for his own use. David responded in anger, "The man who did this deserves to die! He must pay for that lamb four times over, because he did such a thing and had no pity" (2 Sam. 12:5-6). Then Nathan informed David that he was the rich man. Gotcha!

A Dual Life

How could David live such a dual life? He was an adulterous murderer on the inside while maintaining the facade of a righteous king on the outside. His inner torment is described in Psalm 32:

Blessed is he whose transgressions are forgiven, whose sins are covered. Blessed is the man whose sin the LORD does not count against him and in whose spirit is no deceit. When I kept silent, my bones wasted away through my groaning all day long. For day and night your hand was heavy upon me; my strength was sapped as in the heat of summer. Then I acknowledged my sin to you and did not cover up my iniquity. I said, "I will confess my transgressions to the LORD"—and you forgave the guilt of my sin (vv. 1-5).

Such is the inner world of those who live in bondage. "There is nothing concealed that will not be disclosed, or hidden that will not be made known" (Matt. 10:26). Secret sin on Earth is open scandal in heaven. God won't let His children live in darkness for long, because He knows their sin will eat them alive.

I once knew a pastor who had a pornography addiction. At a pastor's conference, some of his colleagues asked for some material he brought with him. As he opened the briefcase with a crowd around him, he suddenly realized he had brought the wrong one. This briefcase had his pornography collection in it! The sham was over.

When I was a pastor, a lady from a previous ministry called for an appointment. She thought her husband was having an affair, but there was no proof. I called her husband and he agreed to see me, but he denied being sexually involved with anyone. Two weeks later, the wife called again and said, "My husband says he has a business trip that will take him out of town for the weekend. I don't believe him. Could I possibly come by and see you again?"

I discerned the husband was lying, but what could I do? There was no proof. All I could think of was the story of David. I related the story to her and suggested we ask God to send him a Nathan. So we prayed together, and she left.

My wife called shortly thereafter and proposed we take our children out for dinner that evening. We went to a little seaport village that had some fine restaurants. Little did I know that I was about to be "Nathan." Low and behold, as we walked into the restaurant, there was the wayward husband with one woman on each arm. He tried to avoid eye contact, but it was too late. He was caught.

I didn't hear from this couple for three years. Then I got a Christmas card from them, thanking me for the time I had spent with them. The husband had asked for and received a job transfer shortly after the embarrassing encounter. Apparently, their marriage is now doing much better.

Sadly, the public lives of many people are radically different from their private lives. As long as they believe the facade can continue, they will not deal with their own issues. Ironically, they are often most critical of others. People who haven't dealt with their own guilt often seek to balance their internal scales by projecting blame on others. But the Lord said in Matthew:

> Do not judge, or you too will be judged. For in the same way you judge others, you will be judged, and with the measure you use, it will be measured to you. Why do you look at the speck of sawdust in your brother's eye and pay no attention to the plank in your own eye? How can you say to your brother, "Let me take the speck out of your eye," when all the time there is a plank in your own eye? You hypocrite, first take the plank out of your own eye, and then you will see clearly to remove the speck from your brother's eye (7:1-5).

Forgiveness and Judgment

David acknowledged his sins, both of which were capital offenses under the law. Then Nathan said, "You are not going to die. But because by doing this you have made the enemies of the Lord [Satan and his angels] show utter contempt, the son born to you will die" (2 Sam. 12:13-14). I don't think we have any idea of the moral outrage our sexual sins cause in the spiritual realm. What we think we are doing privately is done openly before the god of this world and his fallen angelic horde! Far worse, our sexual sins are an offense to God, who is grieved by our failure.

Judgment would come on the household of David. Nathan said to David, "This is what the LORD says: 'Out of your own household I am going to bring calamity upon you. Before your very eyes I will take your wives and give them to one who is close to you, and he will lie with your wives in broad daylight. You did it in secret, but I will do this thing in broad daylight before all Israel'" (2 Sam. 12:11).

After hearing Nathan's story of the rich man who had stolen the sheep, David had demanded that the man should pay fourfold. He didn't know he was speaking of himself. Four of his sons died prematurely. Bathsheba's son died, and another son, Amnon, raped his sister. Amnon was then killed by Absalom, another of David's sons, for raping his sister. Absalom would then "lay with his father's concubines in the sight of all Israel" (16:22) and be killed because he wanted to take the throne from David. Finally, Adonijah, another brother, was executed because he also wanted to become king (see 1 Kings 2:25).

The Lord spared David, but why did Bathsheba's child have to die? Recall that the law did say God would visit "the iniquity of the fathers on the children, on the third and the fourth generations of those who hate Me" (Exod. 20:5, *NASB*). Is it possible that God had to cut off the rebellious seed that was sown? The first male offspring of this adulterous relationship could not receive the birthright. Remember, this is the throne of David upon which the Messiah would someday reign. But God is merciful. He took the infant home to be with Him, and David had the assurance he would be with the child in eternity (see 2 Sam. 12:23).

Warning Against Sexual Immorality

Paul offers the following instruction and warning against sexual immorality:

> The body is not meant for sexual immorality, but for the Lord, and the Lord for the body. By his power God raised the Lord from the dead, and he will raise us also. Do you not know that your bodies are members of Christ himself? Shall I then take the members of Christ and unite them with a prostitute? Never! Do you not know that he who unites himself with a prostitute is one with her in body? For it is said, "The two will become one flesh." But he who unites himself with the Lord is one with him in spirit.
>
> Flee from sexual immorality. All other sins a man commits are outside his body, but he who sins sexually sins against his own body. Do you not know that your body is a temple of the Holy Spirit, who is in you, whom you have received from God? You are not your own; you were bought at a price. Therefore honor God with your body (1 Cor. 6:13-20).

This passage teaches that we have more than a spiritual union with God. Our "bodies are members of Christ himself" (v. 15). Paul said, "If the Spirit of him who raised Jesus from the dead is living in you, he who raised Christ from the dead will also give life to your mortal bodies through his Spirit, who lives in you" (Rom. 8:11). Our bodies are actually temples of God, because His Spirit dwells in us. To use our bodies for sexual immorality is to defile God's temple.

It is difficult for us to fully appreciate the moral outrage of uniting a member of Christ with a prostitute. It would be like Antiochus Epiphanes slaughtering a pig on the altar after declaring Mosaic ceremonies illegal and then erecting a statue of Zeus in the holy place of the Temple. Can you imagine how God's people must have felt when that very thing happened in the second century before Christ? Many were martyred as they attempted to stop the defilement of the Temple.

As a Christian, aren't you offended when people suggest that Jesus was sexually intimate with Mary Magdalene? I am! It also offends me when people suggest Jesus masturbated. I believe Jesus was fully God and also fully man. I believe He was sexually a man and was tempted in all ways such as we are, but that He never sinned. His earthly body was not meant for sexual immorality, and neither is ours. If our eyes were fully open to the reality of the spiritual world and we understood the consequences of sinning against our own bodies, we would obey Scripture and flee from sexual immorality.

Alive in Christ

The apostle Paul taught that we are alive in Christ and therefore identified with Him in His death, burial and resurrection (see Rom. 6:1-11). Because Christ triumphed over sin and death, we have as well, for we are in Christ. The law of life in Christ Jesus has set us free from the law of sin and the law of death (see 8:2). Therefore, Paul said:

> In the same way, count yourselves dead to sin but alive to God in Christ Jesus. Therefore do not let sin reign in your mortal body so that you obey its evil desires. Do not offer the parts of your body to sin, as instruments of wickedness, but rather offer yourselves to God, as those who have been brought from death to life; and offer the parts of your body to him as instruments of righteousness (6:11-13).

Can you think of a way you could commit a sexual sin and not use your body as an instrument of wickedness? I can't. If we commit sexual sins, we allow sin to reign in our mortal bodies. We also lose a degree of freedom and damage our relationships with God. "For you were called to freedom, brethren; only do not turn your freedom into an opportunity for the flesh, but through love serve one another" (Gal. 5:13, *NASB*). What happens when a child of God, who is one spirit with the Lord, unites himself with a prostitute and becomes one flesh with her? Let me illustrate.

How many times have you heard of a nice Christian girl getting involved with an immoral man, having sex with him and then continuing in a sick relationship for years? Her friends try to tell her, "He's no good for you." Mom and Dad abhor the idea that he could be a future son-in-law, but she won't listen to them. Even though he treats her badly, she won't leave him. Why doesn't she just get away from him? Because they've bonded. They have become one flesh.

A pastor asked for my help with a young lady in his congregation. He said, "If you can't help this girl, she is going to be admitted to a hospital. The voices in her head are so loud, she's wondering why we cannot hear them." Being inexperienced with resolving spiritual conflicts, he didn't know whether he was supposed to nail down the chairs in his office or what! It was the classic scenario: A girl gets involved with an immoral man—in this case, a drug dealer—who sexually uses her.

I remember asking the young lady, "If I said you had to leave that guy, what would you say?" She responded, "I'd probably leave right now." I didn't want to ask her to do that until we had a chance to work through the "Steps to Freedom in Christ," so I said, "We are not going to deal with that relationship right now. Instead, because we have this time together, can we help you resolve some of your problems?"

After hearing her story, I asked her if she would be willing to walk through the Steps. During the process, she asked God to reveal to her mind every sexual use of her body as an instrument of unrighteousness. As the Lord brought one experience after another to her mind, she renounced each one. Then she committed her body to the Lord as a living sacrifice. After she had submitted herself to God and resisted the devil, there were no more voices in her head, and she experienced mental peace for the first time in years. I never brought up her boyfriend's name, but she did. "I'm never going to see him again," she said. She left her pastor's office, free in Christ.

In helping others find their freedom in Christ, I have learned through much experience to have them ask the Lord to reveal every sexual use of their bodies as instruments of unrighteousness. Many will openly share one or two sexual experiences during a normal counseling process, but when they sincerely pray that prayer, all the other sexual experiences come to their minds. Why? Because God is the One who grants repentance, which leads to a knowledge of the truth and sets captives free (see 2 Tim. 2:24-26).

A hurting mother and father asked if I would talk with their daughter. Usually nothing good comes from appointments made by parents for their children who don't want to be helped. But I agreed to see their child under the condition that their daughter wanted to see me. They assured me she did, but her opening statement was, "I don't want to get right with God or anything like that!"

Hiding my own frustration, I said to her, "That is certainly your choice, but now that we are together, maybe we could try to resolve some of the conflicts you are in." She said she thought that would be okay.

She told me her story of being date-raped by the campus "hero" while in high school. At the time, she was too embarrassed to tell anyone about this supposedly wonderful boy who had used her body as an instrument of unrighteousness. She had no idea how to resolve it. This was a bad date from the beginning, and she knew it. But how does a star-struck underclassman say no to a superstar upperclassman?

Having lost her virginity, she became sexually promiscuous. Eventually, she lived off and on with a real loser. It was tearing up her parents and their Christian home. She told me about the rape and a little about the last guy.

Then I asked her if she would prayerfully ask the Lord to reveal to her mind every sexual use of her body as an instrument of unrighteousness.

"That would be embarrassing," she said.

"Would you feel better if I waited outside?" I asked.

She said yes, thinking that she could work through it better if I were not there. So I stepped outside while my female prayer partner helped her through it. This young lady sang in church that night for the first time in years. She was free.

Far-Reaching Consequences

After years of helping people find their freedom in Christ, I have observed several commonalities. First, if people have had "unholy" sex, they don't seem to enjoy "holy" sex. I have counseled many wives who loathe being touched by their husbands. In extreme cases, they are actually repulsed by the idea until they break the bondages that come from sex outside God's will. Incredibly, their feelings toward their spouses change almost immediately after finding their freedom in Christ. One pastor hadn't had sex with his spouse for 10 years. To his surprise—and that of his wife—he asked for and had intimate relations with her after attending one of our conferences.

We have also noticed that promiscuity before marriage leads to a lack of fulfillment after marriage. The fun and excitement of sex outside the will of God leaves one in bondage. If premarital sex was entered into with both partners' consent, the bondages only increase as they attempt to satisfy their lusts. If it was without consent (by that I mean sex was forced or the unwilling partner went along with it but didn't really want to), they shut down and remain in bondage to their pasts until resolution is achieved. They lack the freedom to enter into mutual expressions of love and trust. We help them by having them renounce those previous sexual uses of their bodies, commit their bodies to God as living sacrifices, and reserve the sexual use of their bodies for their spouses only.

Imagine the consequences unbridled promiscuity will have on future generations and marriages. Most people have been sexually active before marriage. Fifty percent of those in their 20s have a sexually transmitted disease. Recall Paul's words: "This is the will of God, your sanctification; that is, that you abstain from sexual immorality; that each of you know how to possess his own vessel in sanctification and honor, not in lustful passion, like the Gentiles who do not know God" (1 Thess. 4:3-5, *NASB*).

A former college student under my ministry was dating a lovely Christian lady. He shared with me a profound thought: "I treat my girlfriend the way I think her future husband would want her to be treated." They are now happily married.

I was speaking about sex to a group of high schoolers at an outreach. A non-Christian was there with his girlfriend. He asked, "If I had sex with my girlfriend, would I later regret it?" What a mature question! But I think there is an even more mature question: "Would my girlfriend later regret it?"

My first attempt at discipling a young college man resulted in nothing. He wrote me off after he heard me talk about sexual purity and freedom. At the time, he was dating one of the nicest young ladies in our group. Two years later, he shared with me that during the time I was trying to disciple him, he was sleeping with several coeds, but not the girl he was dating. No wonder our discipleship process wasn't going anywhere! Here was his question: "I get tired of sexual partners in a short time. If I married this young Christian virgin, would I also get tired of her in a short time?"

I told him that what he was tired of was impersonal sex. People who are bored with sex have depersonalized it. He had no relationship with his partners. They were just sex objects to be conquered and used for his own pleasure. He was not thinking of them, just of himself. He was trying to satisfy his lust, but it couldn't be satisfied. The more he fed his appetites, the greater they grew. People such as this become obsessed with sexual thoughts. Obsessional sex is always depersonalized, so boredom increases and the obsessive thoughts grow stronger.

One man told me that masturbation was okay for him because he visualized girls without heads! I told him that was precisely the problem with what he was doing. He was depersonalizing sex. That is also what pornography does. The sex objects are never presented as people created in the image of God, much less some mother's child or brother's sister. To treat the opposite sex as something less than who they really are is to transgress and demean them.

Getting Ready for Marriage

I used to ask young couples in premarital counseling to turn their chairs back to back. I then asked them to write their responses to several questions, such as "How many children do you want to have?" and "When do you want to start having them?" The last question was, "Have you had sexual intercourse with each other?" Eighteen of the first 20 Christian couples I married had already slept together.

Why did I ask? I wanted to know if that was all they had going for them. Did they believe they had to get married because they had sex together? I wanted to know if the woman in the relationship was pregnant, because that would greatly affect the way I discussed issues related to sexual adjustment with them. I also wanted to know what they wanted to tell their children someday about this behavior. I wanted to know if they would be willing to stop until they got married. Were they bringing a load of guilt to the altar? "God has not called us for the purpose of impurity, but in sanctification" (1 Thess. 4:7, *NASB*). We need to get people ready for marriage by getting them right with God.

When the relationships we have with God and our spouses are the most important ones in our lives, sex becomes the most intimate and vulnerable means of expressing love. This vulnerability must not be exploited. We must teach our young men to respect their wives and take care of them. When women can trust their husbands and know that they will be taken care of, they can abandon themselves to sexual pleasures. In fact, trust may be the most important factor determining orgasmic capacity in women.

For some sick reason, our culture is bent on finding the ultimate sexual experience. If people found it, would they be satisfied? Why aren't we instead bent on finding the ultimate personal relationship? "Blessed are those who hunger and thirst for righteousness, for they shall be satisfied" (Matt. 5:6, *NASB*).

What about you? Would you be willing to commit yourself to live a righteous life and pursue the greatest of all relationships, the one every child of God can have with his or her heavenly Father? If so, you will be satisfied, and chances are the sexual relationship you have with your spouse will be satisfying.

A committed Christian couple asked for help at one of my conferences. Because we always try to resolve individual problems first, our lead male encourager met with the husband while I met with the wife. Technically, they professed to be virgins when they got married. However, both had had long-term dating relationships with other people—relationships that had included a lot of heavy petting. The lead male encourager and I sensed God's leading to have them renounce all the physical contact they had had before marriage as though they had bonded to their first love.

The next day the wife, with tears of joy in her eyes, said to me, "Last night was the most wonderful time my husband and I have ever had together."

That is what God wants for your marriage.

Group Discussion

1. What makes lust different from love?

2. Why can't lust be satisfied, and what happens if you try to satisfy it?

3. What in our society panders to our lust?

4. How can we "lust proof" our homes?

5. How should knowing that our bodies are temples of God prevent us from defiling them?

Devotional Guide for Couples

Read Hebrews 13:4 and then share with the other person what violates your conscience.

THE SNAKEBITE OF ADULTERY

The LORD said to Moses, "Make a snake and put it up on a pole; anyone who is bitten can look at it and live." So Moses made a bronze snake and put it up on a pole. Then when anyone was bitten by a snake and looked at the bronze snake, he lived.

NUMBERS 21:8-9

Just as Moses lifted up the snake in the desert, so the Son of Man must be lifted up, that everyone who believes in him may have eternal life. For God so loved the world that he gave his one and only Son, that whoever believes in him shall not perish but have eternal life. For God did not send his Son into the world to condemn the world, but to save the world through him. Whoever believes in him is not condemned, but whoever does not believe stands condemned already because he has not believed in the name of God's one and only Son.

JOHN 3:14-18

A mission church in France decided that women were best taught by a woman and men were best taught by a man. So they had a female adult Sunday School class and a male adult Sunday School class. Both brought their own perspective to the Creation account. Marie taught that God created the man first, but then looked at what He had made and said, "I can do better than that." So He created woman!

Pierre also taught that God created man first, and that all was peaceful and quiet. But it was too quiet. So He created woman. Neither God nor man has had peace or quiet ever since!

Meanwhile, Jean was teaching a mixed group of college students about creation, focusing more on the idea that God created us male and female. In the French language, nouns are designated as either masculine or feminine. One of the students asked what gender should be assigned to a computer. So Jean split the class into two groups—male and female—and asked them to decide for themselves whether "computer" should be a masculine or a feminine noun. The men's group decided that "computer" should definitely be of the feminine gender (*la computer*) because:

- No one but their creator understands their internal logic;
- The native language they use to communicate with other computers is incomprehensible to everyone else;
- Even the smallest mistake is stored in long-term memory for possible later review; and

- As soon as you make a commitment to one, you find yourself spending half your salary on accessories for it

The women's group, however, concluded that computers should be masculine (*le computer*) because:

- In order to do anything with them, you have to turn them on;
- They have a lot of data, but still can't think for themselves;
- They are supposed to help you solve problems, but half the time they *are* the problem; and
- As soon as you commit to one, you realize that if you had waited a little longer, you could have gotten a better model.

The ladies won (again!). The men simply sighed and said, "Women. We can't live with them, and we can't live without them!" Yet these humorous stories point to the fact that men are looking for the perfect wife and women are looking for the perfect husband.

The Perfect Wife

Hardly anyone abandons a perfect wife or a perfect husband for someone else. "Husbands, love your wives," says the Bible (Eph. 5:25). That's easy enough *if* she's always lovable, and *if* . . .

- She's a great cook, serving delicious desserts, and can still fit into her wedding dress.
- She's active at church, PTA, hospital auxiliary and has unlimited time for her husband and children.
- She cares for everyone who is sick in the family and never gets sick herself.

- She has a great sense of humor and never has any bad moods.
- She admires and praises her husband and never nags him about his faults.
- She comes home from work, straightens the house, solves the kids' problems, cooks dinner, gets the homework going, cleans up after dinner, starts the laundry, gets the kids back to their homework, runs to the store, irons, gets the kids to bed, talks with her husband, gets the kids back to bed, folds and puts away the laundry, tidies up the house and still brims with so much energy that she slips into some inviting lingerie to entice her husband to bed for a passionate night.
- She spends an hour each day in prayer and Bible study, yet never appears more knowledgeable than her husband.
- She runs an on-time taxi service for sports practice, piano lessons, ball games, school plays and church programs, and always joins her husband in his many recreational activities.
- She plans great birthday parties for children, parents and all the relatives; special social events; fun weekend getaways; surprises for close friends; wonderful vacations—and never exceeds the family budget.
- She is always improving herself, continuing in education, growing in Bible study, learning computer skills, developing her talents, advancing in her career and always has time to put her husband and children first in everything.
- She tithes, pays all the bills on time, buys food, clothes, furniture, appliances, cars, a dozen insurance policies and still puts away money in the bank, with cash left in her purse to eat out on demand.
- She grooms neatly, dresses attractively, smiles genuinely, exercises regularly, eats modestly and has an ideal weight.

The Perfect Husband

Older women are to teach younger women to love their husbands, which is relatively easy, *if*...

- He makes lots of money and never becomes a workaholic.
- He fixes everything around the house and never botches the job.
- He remembers his anniversary, wife's birthday, kids' birthdays, in-laws' birthdays, engagement day, first date day, special "just for the two of us" days and every other day.
- He sends flowers, cards, notes and little gifts; arranges surprise romantic get-away-alone weekends; and never gives a can opener to his wife on their anniversary.
- He brags about his wife's cooking and is always ready to take her out for dinner.
- He is a creative lover—sensitive, romantic, warm but never pushy or demanding—and always tuned in to his wife's intimate feelings, never thinking about his own desires.
- He is capable, competent, responsible, often elevated to positions of leadership and honor, and never works more than 40 hours per week.
- He goes to all the kids' ball games, plays, lessons and programs but still spends hours sharing his deepest feelings with his wife.
- He has a great sense of humor, is fun to be around and always knows just when to switch to an in-depth conversation.
- He's strong, courageous, tough when needed and never gets angry.
- He's kind, tender, gentle, open, honest, vulnerable and never withdraws or gets his feelings hurt.
- He always cherishes his spouse, showering her with affection and love in all the special ways she dreams about—and never, never disappoints her.

We're pretty sure those lists didn't exactly describe your spouse, and that the only successful method for creating an ideal spouse is to become one yourself! However, that is not going to happen in this lifetime. We are imperfect people marrying imperfect people, and that is why God had sanctification in mind when a man and woman unite in holy matrimony and why marriage is a covenant and committed relationship.

Courting Temptation

When we marry, we fully intend to honor our vows and love our spouses. But our resolve to be faithful weakens whenever we look at someone else of the opposite sex and begin to think, *I wonder what it would be like to be married to him or her.* From that time on, everything is pure fantasy. Of course, we don't have a clue what it would be like to be married to that other person. What people appear to be in public is often quite different from what they are at home.

Take for instance the boss who has the perfect secretary. She is instantly obedient and looks after his every need. So he starts to think what it would be like to be married to her. His wife has stretch marks from giving birth to three children, and her body never returned to the model he married. His secretary is shapely, neat and appears to be a lot less needy than his wife who is burdened down with domestic duties that never end. So he divorces his wife and marries his secretary who is younger, firmer and less demanding. He wakes up the first morning after the honeymoon and asks her to get him a cup of coffee, and she says, "Get it yourself. I'm not your secretary anymore."

When young couples get married, they are making a commitment to one another until death separates them. They should also be instructed not to entertain thoughts contrary to that commitment, because they will all be tempted with such thoughts. People can and do actually carry on affairs in their minds when they think lustful thoughts toward another person, and they will start to bond emotionally and/or sexually to that person. This can lead to stalking, voyeurism and adultery. Consider the wisdom of James 1:13-15 (*NASB*):

> Let no one say when he is tempted, "I am being tempted by God"; for God cannot be tempted by evil, and He Himself does not tempt anyone. But each one is tempted when he is carried away and enticed by his own lust. Then when lust has conceived, it gives birth to sin; and when sin is accomplished, it brings forth death.

Christians are needy people who should be growing every day in Christ. A Christian marriage should foster this growth. We accept one another just as Christ has accepted us, and then by His grace, we love one another. We do this by understanding our spouse's needs and doing all we can to meet them. But we are incapable of meeting the deep longings that only Christ can satisfy. Christ gives us freedom, grace and truth. He satisfies our God-given longings to be accepted, secure and significant. That is why we must put Christ at the center of our own lives as well as our marriages. We cannot expect our spouse to meet a need that only Christ can meet. However, many needs are intended to be met in loving and committed relationships.

Willard F. Harley, Jr., in his book *His Needs, Her Needs,* compares meeting needs to making deposits in our spouse's love banks. Every time we do something good that the other person enjoys, we rank a point.[1] As you would suspect, men and women often calculate differently. Women give one point for each item, no matter how big or small. Men give more points for big items and fewer for small ones. A woman may award one point for a single rose in a vase and also one point for a dozen roses. A man may award one point for a gentle response when he expected a lecture, but four points when his wife gives him a surprise weekend getaway. Of course, the whole idea of a point system is artificial—depositing love units into our spouse's love banks is the important factor.

We can also make withdrawals. Unhappy experiences and disappointing times lead to love units being subtracted from the bank. Continuous effort must be invested to keep each other's love banks overflowing. That is precisely what Christ's love does for us. It keeps flowing through us to others, especially to those in our own families. For this reason, our adversary focuses on marriages and families as his primary targets. He growls in pleasure when we rack up a lot of withdrawals.

How can we make deposits in our spouse's love banks? We can start by meeting their most urgent needs. Harley suggests 10 of these, 5 for wives and 5 for husbands. The 5 strongest needs of wives are affection, conversation, honesty and openness, financial support and family commitment. The 5 strongest needs of husbands are sexual fulfillment, recreational companionship, an attractive wife, domestic support and admiration. Both men and women have all 10 needs, but the order of urgency varies from person to person. Look over the list of all 10 with your spouse and then each rank them in the order of your personal preference.[2]

Prevention is better than cure. Keeping our marriages strong is the best single tactic for making them "affair resistant." Nevertheless, it's not foolproof. Even some marriages that were at one time strong and healthy are being marred by adultery. Personal carnality and the social decline of morality make many spouses vulnerable targets for the adversary.

Snakebites

This is Earth, not heaven. It is a fallen world, not an ideal one. Every Christian must watch out for "that ancient serpent, who is the devil, or Satan" (Rev. 20:2). It is not by accident that the Bible calls Satan a serpent. He is as venomous as a rattlesnake.

Neil lived in Arizona, where the desert is a natural habitat for rattlesnakes. In five years, he experienced six rattlesnakes on his property. Moving them was beyond his expertise (and desire), so he destroyed them to protect his family and pet dog. Long-time residents know that you should cut off the head of the snake and bury it. Even after death, rattlesnakes retain a reflex ability to strike.

Rattlesnakes camouflage themselves very well. They are deadly and silent to the natural senses. People walk by them all the time without realizing they are there. It does no good to relocate them, as they will just come back. You have to strike the head, which is exactly what Christ did. Satan is disarmed, but his venom is still deadly for those who believe his lies.

Paul wrote, "The Spirit clearly says that in later times some will abandon the faith and follow deceiving spirits and things taught by demons" (1 Tim. 4:1). That is happening all over the world at this present time. The devil seeks to divide our mind, because as a double-minded people, we will be unstable in all we do (see Jas. 1:8). He also seeks to divide our marriages, because a house divided against itself cannot stand.

Paul also wrote, "I am afraid that just as Eve was deceived by the serpent's cunning, your minds may somehow be led astray from your sincere and pure devotion to Christ" (2 Cor. 11:3). If we fail to take every thought captive to the obedience of Christ (see 2 Cor. 10:5), we will likely fall away from the faith, destroying our own lives and marriages.

Tempting thoughts must be stopped immediately, or we will suffer some negatives consequences. The problem is that we see the result and not the cause:

- Pornography is not the snake; it's the snakebite.
- Abortion is not the snake, but its bite.
- Adultery is not the snake, but its lethal poison.

Trying to stop abortion and adultery is like trying to push down humps of a snake. You push down one hump and up comes another. We need to stop such problems at the source and win the battle for our minds.

Whoever sows a thought, reaps an action;
Whoever sows an action, reaps a habit;
Whoever sows a habit, reaps a lifestyle;
Whoever sows a lifestyle, reaps a destiny.

Understanding our own sinful condition is difficult to grasp for four reasons. First, we have all been personally involved in sin and live in an environment conditioned by sin. It is very difficult to fully grasp the difference between living in sin and living righteously, because we have never experienced perfect righteousness.

Second, our understanding is skewed by our own sinfulness. We often think less of our sin than we should in order to excuse ourselves. Rather than confess our sin, we rationalize it: "Well, everybody does it!" or "I'm not as bad as that person." Self-righteous people don't seem to realize that to God, their righteousness is like a dirty rag (see Isa. 64:6).

Third, our awareness of what is sinful can easily grow dull with tolerance and exposure to it. The profanity and explicit sex commonly accepted today in television and movies would never have been tolerated 50 years ago. I'm not sure who said the following, but it is well said:

Sin is a monster of such awful mein;
That to be hated, need not to be seen;
But seen too oft, familiar with face;
We first endure, then pity, then embrace.

Fourth, no person has yet experienced the full weight of sin's consequences. Remember, secret sin on Earth is open scandal in heaven. There is nothing being concealed that won't be revealed. Scripture clearly teaches that payday is coming. What we sow we shall someday reap. Yet we often seem oblivious to that truth. Certainly, fictional movies and television contribute to our own delusion. James Bond can hop in and out of bed and his partners never get pregnant—and he never gets a sexually transmitted disease. What a lie! If you get too close to the flame, you will get burned. "Bad company corrupts good morals" (1 Cor. 15:33, *NASB*).

What kind of flawed thinking reasons that we can play with deadly snakes without getting bitten? What makes us think we can charm the snakes? The devil specializes in deception. He has even deceived Christians into thinking that snakebites happen without snakes! The truth is that "we know that we are children of God, and that the whole world is under the control of the evil one" (1 John 5:19) because he has deceived the whole world (see Rev. 12:9).

If you think you can't be deceived or fall into sin as a believer, consider the following testimony:

> I was raised in what everyone thought was the perfect home. My parents were Christians and pillars of the church. They went out of their way to demonstrate their love.
>
> When I reached puberty, I was interested in sex just like every other red-blooded boy. My parents were not very good at sex education, so much of what I learned came from a book they had in our house. From that book I learned to masturbate, and pretty soon I became a slave to masturbation. I found some pornography and became a slave to it. I was in my own private world. On the outside I was a good Christian boy, involved in youth group, a counselor at Christian camps, and a member of the "perfect family" at church. On the inside, I was in complete bondage to pornography and lustful thinking. Magazines, adult book stores, peep shows, movie theaters—you name it, I saw it.

I went to a Christian college, where I continued to feed my lustful habits. I knew the stores that sold pornography, and I would justify my going there.

I married a beautiful Christian woman, and to everyone around us, we were the perfect couple. But I still had this private world that my wife didn't even know about. I got a job that involved a lot of travel, which made it easier to feed my habit. It continued to escalate, and I got closer and closer to the edge (adultery). I always thought that I could dabble with pornography but never commit the "big one." Well, of course it happened, and then it happened again and again. All the while I knew it was wrong, but I couldn't stop. I would feel guilty and remorseful, but I never truly repented.

Finally, events that I know were orchestrated by God led to my wife finding out about what I had done, and I finally confessed to her and to God my life of bondage to pornography and sex. I fell to my knees before God and repented of my sin, and for the first time I truly felt the love and grace of God. With the help of your books, *Victory Over the Darkness*, *The Bondage Breaker* and *Finding Freedom in a Sex-Obsessed World*, I was able to discover my identity and freedom in Christ. Never before have I felt such freedom. No more bondage! No more slavery to sin!

My wife has struggled through this with me and we received some pretty intense counseling. Praise God we are doing better than we ever have, and Christ is finally the center of our home and the center of my life.

Not Me!

Too many Christians think to themselves, *This couldn't happen to me! I know God's Word. I teach it (and even preach it) to my friends. I'm outspoken against immorality. There's no way I'm going to fall.* Christians who believe they are immune are setting themselves up for temptation. The greater the denial, the easier the deception. Little compromises sneak up on them. They treat the snakes as if they were domesticated and no threat at all. In fact, they may not even recognize danger until it's too late.

Yet the truth is that we all need to heed Paul's advice:

Therefore let him who thinks he stands take heed that he does not fall. No temptation has overtaken you but such as is common to man; and God is faithful, who will not allow you to be tempted beyond what you are able, but with temptation will provide the way of escape also, so that you may be able to endure it (1 Cor. 10:12-13).

Be aware of vulnerable moments during times of stress and life transitions such as midlife crisis. For instance, temptations often come during business travel when a spouse is simply missing a conversational companion. Along comes a "nice" person who is willing to talk and listen, and one compromise leads to another until it is too late to take the way of escape. The believer hates it later, feeling the guilt of betraying the Lord and a faithful spouse.

Such failures during vulnerable times are more likely if there is a hidden pornography habit and/or unresolved marital conflict. The evil one attacks at the weakest point and produces *diminishing respect*. He whispers his thoughts into the person's mind, usually in the first person singular, "I":

- I'm depressed all the time. I'm so tired of being unhappy.
- I hate this marriage. I don't want to go on like this. Am I going to spend the rest of my life this way?
- It just isn't fair, because . . .
- Look at him! (Look at her!) How can I respect someone like that?
- I just don't want to be married anymore.

When diminishing respect connects with increasing expectations, danger intensifies. One of the subtle dangers in any marriage is that people gradually expect more and more from their spouses. Often the expectations swirl around finances, with demands to earn more or spend less. The expectations may touch other sensitive subjects, such as sex, time together, communication or parenting. As pressures and expectations rise, they are accompanied by the disillusionment that things will never change, now or ever. People begin to rationalize:

- I'm putting more into this marriage than I'm getting out of it.
- I'm tired of living with my nose to the grindstone. When are you going to get a raise? or When will you stop squandering our money?
- You always . . . !
- You never . . . !
- Why don't you . . . ?

The couple experiences a breakdown in sensitive communication and intimate relationships. Morning conversations may sound something like the following:

"Please pass the toast."

"What's the weather supposed to be today?"

"I'm late for work, so I need to hurry."

The couple is talking mind to mind but not heart to heart. No real feelings flow between them. They act more like business partners than lovers. At night, their sexual relationship reflects the same neglect, boredom or frustration. They are too busy, too tired, too disinterested or, conversely, too demanding, too demeaning, too dissatisfied.

Stages of Adultery

Suppose a spouse is feeling trapped in a marriage when along comes a person of the opposite sex, usually separated or divorced, and available. This person listens and empathizes. So the two just talk; that's all. What's wrong with that? Both would say they are just friends, nothing more. Intimate communication is taking place with the opposite sex *outside* the marriage, but it's not occurring *inside* the marriage. These two naïve people have just entered the first of three stages, *the conversation stage*.

The Conversation Stage

The relationship progresses with emotional delight and innocent touching. If he is her friend, she may give him a social hug or an embrace to say goodbye. If she is his secretary, he may put his hand on her shoulder while giving instructions.

A man shared with his pastor that he was feeling strongly attracted to his secretary and feeling absolutely nothing for his wife. The wise pastor asked, "How often are you touching your secretary?"

"Oh, I'm not touching her at all," he replied.

"This week you keep track of any way at all that you touch her," the pastor challenged him.

A week later the man reported, "I'm touching her all the time, and I'm liking it, too."

A mere social hug may be a good thing. But when the hug is with the person with whom the tender talk and emotional delight are also occurring, yellow caution lights should start flashing. If you're looking forward to the next hug, you're in trouble!

The Friendship Stage

The relationship has now entered the *friendship stage*. If asked, both would say, "We're just good friends." They are still in denial and are being deceived.

I was privileged to serve on a panel for a Focus on the Family radio broadcast with Dr. James Dobson. The other panel members included two couples who had rebuilt their marriages after adultery. With one couple, the wife had fallen into an adulterous affair; with the other couple, it was the husband.

For their children's sakes, the couples preferred not to use their real names. The couple in which the wife had committed adultery went by the names of Judy and Peter. The couple lived in an upscale neighborhood, attended an evangelical church regularly and knew Christ as Lord and Savior. They were friends and business associates with the couple who lived next door. They played tennis together, had dinners together and were generally the best of friends.

Peter then contracted hepatitis, but gradually recovered. Judy did not understand that a period of depression sometimes follows the disease. Although they previously had a good marriage, Peter was not presently much fun to live with, and Judy didn't know why.

Judy and her male neighbor spent more and more time together talking. She even tried to help him talk through some of his marriage problems. The two couples were again having dinner together. In their social circle, it was not unusual for husband and wife to be sitting across the table from each other. So Judy was seated beside the other man. During the evening, his hand reached over and touched hers, lingering for just a moment.

"In that moment," Judy said, "I knew I loved him." It was not long before their relationship progressed and resulted in an adulterous affair.

The Belonging Stage

Leaving Judy and Peter and returning to our hypothetical but typical couple, the relationship that began in the conversation stage and progressed in the friendship stage now accelerates into the *belonging stage*. The two begin to spend hidden times together.

Unbeknownst to their spouses, they start making personal time or misusing company time in order to be together. Meeting in secret often requires covering up the truth or lying. They begin making phone calls, sending notes or cards, and giving personal gifts to each other. However, because they are not sleeping together, they deny this is an affair. They just know that they are close friends. If you asked them if they were having an emotional affair—and received an honest answer—they might say, "Well, yes, you might call it that."

The woman in the relationship begins to assess what is really going on. If she's married and a Christian, she may reason, *I made a mistake about the man I married. He really wasn't God's will for me.*

The man may think, *I'm in love with two women. I love my wife and I love this woman. What am I supposed to do? But I am responsible for getting her into this relationship, so I can't hurt her* [the woman in the emotional affair, not his wife].

The emotional pressure and physical temptation now feel overwhelming. The warning lights are flashing red, but the couple no longer notices. They do what they thought at one time would never happen. That's what happened to Judy and the man next door. That's what happens to thousands of Christians who fall into denial and deception. They get bitten by the snake, and nothing will ever be the same again.

Usually, the adultery stays hidden for a while, but eventually the two are found out. Sometimes, the affair gets broken off. The tragic story ends in divorce court with finances devastated, children emotionally damaged, and a cycle of adultery and divorce that may become a pattern for the next three or four generations.

Breaking Off an Adulterous Affair

Judy and Peter, the two panelists on Focus on the Family, were among the blessed ones. They saved their marriage.

Peter had begun to grow suspicious. He couldn't quite articulate the problem, but he knew things were not right. He thought it strange that Judy spent so much time talking to his neighbor and business partner, although they were best of friends. But then, the neighbor needed some help, and Judy was adept at helping people.

Meanwhile, Judy was lying to cover her tracks. The affair and the cover-up that accompanied it were taking an emotional toll on her. She was seeing both her pastor and a psychologist for counseling, though she was not telling either of them the whole story.

As Peter's suspicions grew, he decided to make an appointment with an attorney friend. He shared with him everything he had seen and felt. Through his law practice, the attorney had met countless couples whose adultery led to divorce. He could easily decipher the signs of adultery. The attorney said, "I don't *think* your wife is having an affair—I *know* she is. Here is my advice. Hire a private investigator to secure the evidence you need before you confront her."

Peter said it was one of the most difficult decisions he ever had to make in his life. Who wants to hire a cop to follow his wife? But he did, and it wasn't long before the facts were known.

Peter was a no-nonsense kind of guy. He filed for divorce first and then confronted his wife (not a recommended practice). Already having second thoughts about the other man, Judy was devastated. She broke off the adulterous affair and threw herself on Peter's mercy—a good strategy.

Judy explained how she felt at that moment, totally broken before God: "I had lied about it until I became so overdosed with lies that I—in absolute brokenness on my knees—said, 'I will never lie again about anything, any time, anywhere. I don't care what the consequences are the rest of my life. I don't ever want to tell another lie, live a double life.' I hated the deception."

Judy kept her word. She never lied to Peter again and never returned to the adultery. By God's grace, Judy's repentance and Peter's faithfulness, they saved their marriage.[3]

What should we do if we discover our spouse is committing adultery? As the faithful spouse—not perfect but faithful—experiencing the pain of an adulterous husband or wife, we should immediately seek counsel from an experienced pastor. Emotions are often too gut-wrenching to permit clear thinking, and every action will have consequences. In any crisis, before taking any action Christians should first pray, search the Scripture, listen to the Holy Spirit and get godly counsel. Then act!

One strategy for the wounded husband or wife is to pray fervently, remove excuses and become the spouse God created you to be. Love can sometimes win where anger will lose.[4] Adulterous affairs blow up faster than marriages. Rising expectations also prevail in an affair, and those hopes and dreams are seldom satisfied outside of marriage. Because most adulterous affairs are built on human weakness and failure, they will usually collapse. If we turn to the Lord for help during our times of greatest pain, we can become more conformed to His image and more like the people God intended us to be.

The faithful spouse should not tolerate a persistent, repeated pattern of adultery. Dr. James Dobson suggests writing a letter to open the cage door and release the partner who feels trapped. With it comes a statement that all services in this marriage will immediately come to an end.[5] Although we never give counsel to divorce, there is a time for taking a stand and showing tough love (see 1 Cor. 7:10-11). This may require separation if that is what it takes to get the other person to seek the help he or she needs.

Act Now

If you are the spouse involved in an adulterous affair, it's past time for you to break it off. Adultery violates the Ten Commandments and brings the judgment of God upon you and your descendants. Whatever pleasure you experience now is not worth it in the face of eternity.

> Sooner or later we'll all have to face God, regardless of our con-
> ditions. We will appear before Christ and take what's coming to
> us as a result of our actions, either good or bad. *That* keeps us
> vigilant, you can be sure. It's no light thing to know that we'll
> all one day stand in that place of Judgment (2 Cor. 5:10-11,
> *THE MESSAGE*, emphasis added*)*.

Neil has helped many adulterous men get right with God by taking them through the Steps to Freedom in Christ. When they are done, he offers the man a phone so that he can call the other woman. He asks the man to make it final right there in his presence. Some will say, "I can't do that now. I owe her something." Of course, the man doesn't owe her anything other than a final goodbye, and the same goes for the woman. He owes his wife and children an apology, restitution and repentance. If he goes to the other woman again in private, you know what will likely happen. As Paul states in 1 Corinthians 10:14, "Therefore, my beloved, flee from idolatry" (*NASB*). Leave forever and never go back.

Three steps are needed to end an adulterous affair and recover from its effects. You must *amputate it, grieve the loss of it* and *heal from the amputation*. Amputation is a painful but essential action. It means you must sever, once and for all, the one-flesh relationship with the adulterous lover (and anyone else except your spouse). Only a total break will do. In that phone conversation, you must say, "We can never see each other again. It's over!"

The next step is to find someone to hold you accountable by his or her presence as you terminate the adulterous relationship. This gives the extra courage you will so desperately need. If this approach is impossible, our counsel is not to visit your lover in person. Use the phone, and then change your phone number. We do not recommend writing a letter, as that can be used against you. Making sure that a future connection is impossible may even require changing jobs or moving to another location.

Amputating an adulterous affair will be painful because the Bible teaches that even sexual intercourse with a prostitute creates a one-flesh bond (see 1 Cor. 6:16). For those who jump from one sexual partner to another without love and commitment, the amputations must be total and simultaneous. At this point, the Bible calls for repentance: true remorse and radical change with a dedication to repair the damage. It also calls for a binding promise to live God's way in the future.

Most people who break off an adulterous affair fail to understand the inevitable grieving process. Christians sometimes wrongly believe that everything will be all right because the adultery has ended. This myth contains three totally wrong beliefs. One is that the marriage will instantly recover. However, because the problems in the marriage built up over a period of years, they will not disappear overnight. Refilling a spouse's love bank takes time.

The second wrong belief is that grieving over the amputated affair will not be necessary. Although the relationship was completely sinful, it did provide some evil substitute satisfactions for what God intended in marriage. A time of grieving is normal, not abnormal. Bouncing back and forth like a ping-pong ball between spouse and the other adulterer never works. Gradual withdrawal only creates more pain and devastation for everyone involved. It's like trying to run on a broken leg.

The third wrong belief is that trust can be immediately reestablished. The injured spouse will hopefully forgive you for the sake of the marriage, but it will take a long time to reestablish trust. This means that you will need to account for the time when you were absent from your forgiving spouse. You will need to prove again that you are trustworthy, and that will take time. To facilitate this process, you should seek the kind of godly counsel that can break the bondage created by your lustful habits.

During the grieving process, set a cast that will not allow you to return to the adulterous affair. The hardness of the cast is a discipline called 24-hour accountability. This means that you give your spouse permission to phone at any time, check up on you anywhere, and ask any questions. Your permission should include an agreement to respond honestly and humbly. The cast, the discipline of accountability, means you will call often and give account of all your time, including where you've been and what you have been doing. Any lying, even "white" lies, must immediately be confessed and abandoned.

Casts are uncomfortable and clumsy. This discipline will go against your former false sense of freedom. It will irk you, because you are being treated like a child. But as you begin to rebuild trust in your partner's eyes, you will find that it is worth it.

Amputees do heal—and so do marriages that survive adultery. Actually, marriages in which adultery has occurred are more common than most people think. For the protection of their children and their reputations, most Christian couples who have survived adultery prefer never to mention it again other than between themselves. In fact, it took Dr. Dobson two years to find people who were willing to tell their stories on the broadcast mentioned earlier in this chapter. Most of the couples he asked to publicly share their personal experiences with recovery from adultery told him, "No thanks."

Thousands of other couples have rebuilt their marriages after adultery, and so can you. Time, effort and godly counsel will be needed. It will take everything you've got to rebuild what was destroyed. But great effort always pays big dividends. All couples who work wholeheartedly on their marriages, with or without an earlier incident of adultery, will experience a great improvement in their relationships.

Finding Hope for Your Marriage

Your story may not be the same as the one described in this chapter. It may be that you are a Christian married to an unfaithful non-Christian who lives by this world's standards. It may be that your spouse indulged in a careless one-night fling and later regretted it deeply. It may be that your spouse is a sexual addict who needs intensive spiritual and psychological counseling.

Freedom in Christ is available for sexual addicts as well as for those who are beguiled by their own denial and Satan's deception. Both the "Personal Steps to Freedom," which can be purchased in Christian bookstores, and the "Marriage Steps to Freedom" explained in chapter 12 of this book will prove helpful to both you and your spouse. Offering forgiveness and breaking sexual bondage are vital for marital healing.

When the Israelites experienced the judgment of a plague of snakes among them, Moses prayed for the people, and God instructed him to raise up a bronze snake on a pole. Anyone who had the faith to look at God's provision lived. The others died. While talking with Nicodemus, Jesus predicted His coming crucifixion as the cure for spiritual snakebites: "Just as Moses lifted up the snake in the desert, so the Son of Man must be lifted up, that everyone who believes in him may have eternal life" (John 3:14-15).

Look at the cross: Jesus died for your sins. Look at the empty tomb: He rose again to give you eternal and spiritual life, hope and a future. Look at the throne of God: Jesus reigns, having crushed the head of the serpent.

Notes
1. Willard F. Harley, Jr., *His Needs, Her Needs, Building an Affair-Proof Marriage* (Grand Rapids, MI: Fleming H. Revell, 1986, 1994), pp. 18-28.
2. Ibid., pp. 179-185.
3. "Marriages that Survived Infidelity," Focus on the Family broadcast, Wednesday, November 1, 1995. Audiocassettes may be ordered from Focus on the Family (1-800-AFAMILY).
4. Charles Mylander, *Running the Red Lights* (Ventura, CA: Regal Books, 1986), pp. 91-113.
5. Dr. James C. Dobson, *Love Must Be Tough, New Hope for Families in Crisis* (Waco, TX: Word Books, 1983), pp. 44-50, 67-69.

Group Discussion

1. Why is it likely that we will be tempted to think about what it would be like to be married to a "better spouse"—someone more attractive or more suitable than the person we're married to?

2. Why is it necessary to take every thought captive to the obedience of Christ?

3. Willard Harley suggests the five most urgent needs of a husband and a wife. Do you agree? What needs would you add or subtract?

4. Why don't we easily see our own sin?

5. Why are we inclined to think the sin of adultery will never happen to us? What is the proper response to such an assumption?

Devotional Guide for Couples

Read and discuss Titus 3:14 and then share with each other your two greatest needs from Harley's list, as follows:

Husband	Wife
Sexual fulfillment	Conversation
Recreational companionship	Openness and honesty
An attractive wife	Affection
Domestic support	Financial support
Admiration	Family commitment

FOR FREEDOM'S SAKE

*Then came Peter to him, and said, Lord, how oft shall my brother sin against
me, and I forgive him? till seven times? Jesus saith unto him, I say not unto thee,
Until seven times: but, Until seventy times seven.*

MATTHEW 18:21-22, *KJV*

*But whom you forgive anything, I forgive also; for indeed what I have forgiven,
if I have forgiven anything, I did it for your sakes in the presence of Christ, in order
that no advantage be taken of us by Satan; for we are not ignorant of his schemes.*

2 CORINTHIANS 2:10-11, *NASB*

*Forgive us our debts, as we also have forgiven our debtors. For if you forgive
men when they sin against you, your heavenly Father will also forgive you. But
if you do not forgive men their sins, your Father will not forgive your sins.*

MATTHEW 6:12,14-15

*Be kind and compassionate to one another, forgiving each other,
just as in Christ God forgave you.*

EPHESIANS 4:32

*Bear with each other and forgive whatever
grievances you may have against one another.
Forgive as the Lord forgave you.*

COLOSSIANS 3:13

According to Royce Frazier, a marriage and family counselor, if you ask a husband or wife "What's your responsibility in marriage?" during their middle years of marriage, most will respond in terms of parenting:

- "I provide for the family. I work hard to give them the best."
- "I work outside the home, but I also cook, clean and take care of the children."
- "I spend a lot of time with the family. The kids' activities really keep us busy."

Fortunate are the children whose parents love and discipline them for the sake of godliness! Good parenting alone, however, is never enough. Troubled children are infected by generational sins and their parents' dysfunctional marriages. Conflict and crisis in marriage affect the whole family. Research on the children of divorce reveals devastating damage when parents permanently separate.[1]

Good marriages produce good children. They provide a model for growth. Nobody can model perfection—that belongs to Christ alone—but children do watch how we handle pressure and conflict. If we don't own up to our mistakes, they won't either. If we lie to protect ourselves, so will they. If we don't forgive one another, it is likely they won't either. Roots of bitterness will rise up and many will be defiled (see Heb. 12:15). For this reason, we would do well to heed the advice Paul gives to those living in the close confinement of committed relationships:

So, as those who have been chosen of God, holy and beloved, put on a heart of compassion, kindness, humility, gentleness and patience; bearing with one another, and forgiving each other, whoever has a complaint against anyone; just as the Lord forgave you, so also should you (Col. 3:12-13, *NASB*).

The Need to Forgive

Many readers will not have to face the trial of forgiving an unfaithful spouse. But all will have to face the setbacks of daily life—baggage from dysfunctional parents, financial pressures, layoffs from work, too little time alone, sex problems, communication breakdowns, miscarriages, premenstrual syndrome, menopause, surgeries, tragedies, rebellious adolescents, interfering in-laws. It's easy to accumulate regrets and resentments while living in this fallen world with imperfect people. In fact, it is natural to seek revenge or be bitter when treated unjustly, but it is divine to forgive 70 times 7 times, if necessary. (If you're counting, you're not forgiving.)

In the Lord's Prayer we are taught to pray, "Father, forgive me as I have forgiven others." This model prayer reveals that our relationship with God is inextricably bound up with our relationship with others. We can't be bitter and unloving to others and be right with God. "If someone says, 'I love God,' and hates his brother, he is a liar; for the one who does not love his brother whom he has seen, cannot love God whom he has not seen" (1 John 4:20, *NASB*).

Chuck and I coauthored a book on reconciliation entitled *Blessed Are the Peacemakers* (Regal Books, 2002). Reconciliation is the ministry God has given to the Church (see 2 Cor. 5:18), and it is critically important for healthy marriages. To be reconciled, the enmity that exists between ourselves and others must be removed. This requires repentance and forgiveness. We are first reconciled to God, which is possible because the enmity of sin that separated us has been dealt with. God did not have to repent, but He did have to find a way to forgive us in order to be reconciled with us.

Reconciliation with God is the basis for living with others. "We love because he first loved us" (1 John 4:19). We are to be merciful to others as He has been merciful to us (see Luke 6:36). We are to forgive as He has forgiven us (see Eph. 4:32). To understand this better, consider three terms: "justice," "mercy" and "grace."

Justice is equity, fairness and rightness. If you meted out justice, you would be giving people what they deserve. If God gave us what we deserved, we would all be assigned to hell. Mercy means not giving people what they deserve. Grace means giving people what they don't deserve. As believers who are reconciled to God, we are to be merciful and not give people what they deserve. But we are not supposed to stop there. We should take the next step and give people what they don't deserve. In other words, we should love one another with the unconditional love of God.

The offended person must forgive if he or she wants to be right with God, but the offender has to repent if reconciliation is going to take place. We don't forgive the other person for that person's sake. We do it for our sake, and initially it is only an issue between ourselves and God. That is why it is vitally important to make a distinction between the need to forgive and the need to seek forgiveness from others.

If we have offended someone else, we need to go to that person, seek his or her forgiveness, and make restitution if possible (see Matt. 5:23-26). According to Jesus, we should leave our offering at church and go seek reconciliation with others when so convicted. But if we need to forgive someone who has offended us, we need to go to God. People often think that they need to go to the offending party in order to forgive that person. This is not true, as in some cases it is impossible to forgive this person due to death or distance, while in other cases it is inadvisable due to potential harm or abuse.

We have had the privilege of helping people all over the world find their freedom in Christ through genuine repentance and faith in God (we do this using The Steps to Freedom in Christ). In every case, forgiveness has been essential for the resolution of their personal and spiritual conflicts. This happens without their seeing or interacting with those who have offended them. In many cases, they are led to seek reconciliation with those they have offended after they have gotten right with God.

Paul wrote, "If it is possible, as far as it depends on you, be at peace with everyone" (Rom. 12:18). But it doesn't always depend on us. If the other person doesn't want to make things right or won't repent, there is nothing we can do about it. But that doesn't mean we can't be right with God. Our freedom does not depend on those people whom we have no right or ability to control.

God doesn't want us to live in bitterness, so if we won't forgive from our hearts, He will turn us over to the enemy for mental torment. In Matthew 18:35, Jesus said, "This [being tortured] is how my heavenly Father will treat each of you unless you forgive your brother from your heart" (v. 35).

Would the heavenly Father let someone be tortured just for not forgiving? To find out, simply try not forgiving. You will be tormented with thoughts toward the other person. It feels like battery acid in the soul. Why would our Father let us go through so much pain? "Because the Lord disciplines those he loves" (Heb. 12:6). If a little pain will lead us to the freedom of forgiveness, He will allow the torment.

Paul urges us to forgive "so that no advantage would be taken of us by Satan, for we are not ignorant of his schemes" (2 Cor. 2:11, *NASB*). "Schemes" is the Greek word *noema* and in 2 Corinthians is translated as "mind" (see 4:4; 11:3) and "thought[s]" (see 10:5). These "thoughts" are often placed in the first person singular, "I":

- I'm not ready to forgive yet.
- I need some counseling first.
- I shouldn't feel this way.
- It's my fault; I don't have anything to forgive.
- It's not that big of a deal; I'll just forget it.
- I'm not going to just let them off my hook!
- Why should I forgive? They're the ones who need to ask my forgiveness.

Nursing a grudge leads to resentment. Resentment smolders into bitterness that pollutes our souls. Bitter people invite trouble, because they blindly cause it. Why don't we instead seriously consider becoming like Christ and let go of the past, grab hold of God's grace and forgive our parents, spouse, friends, associates, neighbors and enemies? God's grace will always enable us to do what He has commanded.

"But why should I let them off the hook?" you may say. That is precisely why you need to forgive them, because you are still hooked to them. Bitterness keeps us bound to the past, but forgiveness sets us free and allows us to move forward. If we let others off our hook, they are still on God's hook. "Never take your own revenge, beloved, but leave room for the wrath of God, for it is written, 'VENGEANCE IS MINE, I WILL REPAY,' says the Lord" (Rom. 12:19). God will deal justly with those who have offended us in His time and in His way.

We are to forgive as Christ has forgiven us. He did that by taking the consequences of our sins upon Himself. Forgiveness is agreeing to live with the consequences of another person's sin. "But that is not fair!" you say. Yes, it isn't fair, but you will have to do it anyway. We are all living with the consequences of someone else's sins. The only real choice is to do that in the bondage of bitterness or the freedom of forgiveness. "But where is the justice?" you ask. The justice is in the Cross. Jesus died once for all for your sins, his sins and her sins.

"I'll just forget about it, the way God does." God couldn't forget if He wanted to because He is omniscient. When He says He will remember our sins no more, He means that He will not take the past and use it against us in the future. He will remove it as far from Him as the East is from the West. When a spouse says, "Two years ago you did such and such," he or she is saying, "I didn't forgive you." That spouse is still bringing up the past and using it against the other person.

While going through the Steps, a young lady said, "I can't forgive my mother. I hate her." I said, "Now you can. God is not asking you to like someone or to ignore your hurt feelings." In order to forgive from our heart, we have to get down to the emotional core before healing can take place. If we forgive generically, we will get generic freedom. To forgive from our heart, we have to be totally honest about how we feel. We can't be right with God and not be real. The first step in any recovery process is to get out of denial and face the truth.

The Grace to Forgive

Jesus didn't have to take upon Himself the sins of a few like we have to. He had to take *all* the sins of the world upon Himself. That same power and grace is now working in us. As we look to the Cross to grasp how the Lord Jesus forgave us, we should consider three passages.

> When they came to the place called the Skull, there they crucified him, along with the criminals—one on his right, the other on his left. Jesus said, "Father, forgive them for they do not know what they are doing" (Luke 23:33-34).

On the cross, Jesus experienced pain and anguish at the hands of those who crucified Him. When we forgive as the Lord forgave us, we experience the pain caused by those who have hurt us. It seems contradictory to experience the pain in order to stop the pain. However, the pain only subsides when the heart releases the offense. Forgiveness takes place with the full acknowledgment of the pain.

There is an old saying, "Time heals all wounds." This is true enough if there is not infection or foreign material in the wounds. But if bitterness or resentment infects the spirit, it is more accurate to say, "Time buries all wounds." Time will eventually bury the pain of old grievances that were never forgiven, but it does not heal them. They are not buried dead; they are buried alive. Without warning, they will crawl out of the pit of our suppressed memories. Unforgiven hurts will rise from the grave to haunt us.

> This is how we know what love is: Jesus Christ laid down his life for us. And we ought to lay down our lives for our brothers (1 John 3:16).

On the cross, Jesus showed suffering love, laying down His life instead of retaliating against those who hurt Him. When we forgive as the Lord forgave us, we show suffering love, laying down our right to get even with those who have hurt us. In cases of battery and abuse, we need to report it—but still forgive. Justice and forgiveness walk hand in hand. This is possible because we ourselves are forgiven children of a just God. Because we belong to a just God, we call on His human authorities on Earth for justice. Because we are children of a forgiving God, we forgive as Christ forgave us.

> For God so loved the world that he gave his one and only Son, that whoever believes in him shall not perish but have eternal life (John 3:16).

On the cross, Jesus let us off the hook and set us free. When we forgive as the Lord forgave us, we let others off our hook and release them to

God's wisdom and judgment. We give up our "right" to get even or settle the score. We leave revenge in God's hands.

When Chuck was a boy, he went fishing with his cousin. During one very bad cast, his fishhook stuck in his cousin's cheek. They couldn't get it out, so they walked to his cousin's house. His mother couldn't get it out either. They went to the doctor. The experienced doctor pushed the tip of the hook on through the cheek, clipped off the barb, and then pulled it out.

The hook in the cousin's cheek was Chuck's fault, because Chuck was the one who had hurt him. But once the hook was in the boy's cheek, it was his hook. It would not turn him loose. Suppose he had said, "I'm not going to let you off my hook." Guess who would have kept hurting?

Suppose Chuck had continued to hold the line and had tugged on it whenever he felt like it. The original offense would have kept hurting his cousin again and again. Chuck wasn't hurting, but his cousin was. The only way for the cousin to get free would be to release the hook. If he refused to let Chuck off his hook, he would keep on hurting. Whoever refuses to forgive prolongs the pain.

> I cannot play the martyr role when I forgive,
> > because Jesus did not forgive me that way.
> I cannot settle the score first before I forgive,
> > because Jesus did not forgive me that way.
> I cannot keep a running tally of grievances,
> > because Jesus did not forgive me that way.
> I cannot forgive with my lips and then bring it up again to
> increase my advantage over others,
> > because Jesus did not forgive me that way.
> I cannot forgive and then tell others about the offense,
> > because Jesus did not forgive me that way.

I cannot go through all the motions of forgiveness and then
harbor resentment for weeks, months, years,
   because Jesus did not forgive me that way.
I can forget the score and erase the tally of rights and wrongs,
   because Jesus forgave me that way.
I can keep loving and respecting the one who hurt me,
   because Jesus forgave me that way.
I can foster genuine repentance,
   because Jesus forgave me that way.
I can take the first step toward reconciliation,
   because Jesus forgave me that way.
I can release the resentment that clings to the past,
   because Jesus forgave me that way.
I can bring healing to a broken relationship,
   because Jesus forgave me that way.
I can be kind, compassionate and forgive another
   just as Christ forgave me (see Eph. 4:31-32).

Forgiveness is a crisis of the will. We choose to forgive from the
heart. That means we let God surface all the painful memories of our
past. The natural tendency is to try to push those memories down, but
they must surface so that we can face the pain and let it go.

Ask the Lord who it is that you need to forgive. For each person's
name that surfaces in your mind, say the prayer below. Stay with each
person until every painful memory has been addressed. Don't say,
"Lord, help me to forgive so and so" or "Lord, I want to forgive so and
so." Rather, say, "Lord, *I* forgive . . ." You are making a choice to forgive
from your heart.

We have found it helpful for some to add something like this:
"Lord, I forgive my father for leaving Mom and us kids, because it made
me feel . . . [then list how it made you feel, such as rejected, unworthy,

unloved]." Saying how a hurtful event made you feel will help you get in touch with your damaged emotions. You don't heal in order to forgive. You forgive in order to heal.

> *Lord, I forgive [name] for [specifically identify all offenses*
> *and painful memories and feelings].*

If you have been severely traumatized, it may help to pray through the following 10 steps, one at a time. Personalize each step by inserting the person's name or recalling the incident.

Ten Steps to Forgiveness

1. *Allow yourself to feel the pain, hurt, resentment, bitterness and hate* (see Matt. 5:4). Avoid the two extremes of "I shouldn't feel that way" and "I'm not ready to forgive yet."

2. *Submit yourself to God, recalling how Christ forgave you* (see Luke 23:33-34; Col. 3:13). Take it to the Cross! That is where you will find justice. People want justice now, but that will never perfectly happen in our lifetime.

3. *Ask for Christ's grace and power to forgive* (see Luke 11:9-10). Jesus understands because He has been there, and He will enable us to forgive.

4. *Agree to live with the unavoidable consequences of the other person's sins against you* (see Eph. 5:21; Col. 3:13). If the consequences are avoidable and it's legal, right and moral to do so, then by all means avoid them! But if the consequences are unavoidable, you will have to live with them anyway. Your only choice is between the bondage of bitterness and the freedom of forgiveness.

5. *Release the offense.* Tear up the debt the other person owes you (see Matt. 6:12). When we pray the Lord's Prayer, "Forgive us our debts as we forgive our debtors," we are not speaking of finances. Tear up the personal, moral and relational debt you feel the other person owes you. This is the heart of forgiveness.

6. *Never bring it up again* (see Rom. 12:17). In marriage, this means that once you forgive, you can never use the information as a weapon during a fight. You can never use the information against your spouse. The subject can be discussed to bring resolution or progress, but you should never say, "Well, do you remember when you . . . ?"

7. *Keep forgiving when your emotions recycle the pain or when the person keeps offending you* (see Matt. 18:21-22). The key to living above the circumstances of life is to not pick up the offense in the first place. That is still true after you have forgiven someone yet that person keeps sinning. Try praying for the person, as he or she is obviously not living in a way that is right. After forgiving major traumas, you can pick up the offense again. This is where you have to win the battle for your mind. The devil will tempt you to think again about the injustices of the past. You have to say, "I'm not going there ever again. I let that go, and I am not going to pick it up again."

   Your emotions will cycle to a low place in which you won't feel like you ever forgave anything in the first place. The adversary will whisper in your mind, "Just look at you! What a hypocrite you are! You feel just the same as you did before. You didn't forgive at all. This forgiveness stuff works for other people, but it doesn't work for you."

That is when you need to submit to God and resist the devil (see Jas. 4:7): "Lord Jesus, I submit my body to you as a living sacrifice. Please fill me with your Holy Spirit. In Your name and by Your authority, I command Satan and all his demons to leave my presence."

If you have picked up the offense and the emotions come back, simply pray the forgiveness prayer once again: "Lord, I forgive [name the person] for [name the offense]." It will take you about half as long as it did the first time. Should you lose the mental battle a second time, the third time will only take half as long as the second time. Soon your emotions will be healed and forgiveness will become a way of life.

8. *Reject the sinful act and tolerate it no longer* (see Rom. 12:21). God does not want you to put up with abuse. Take your stand against the sin. If necessary, find godly allies in your church or get help from someone with governmental authority to stand with you. You have every right to set up scriptural boundaries to stop further abuse. You will never help the abuser by allowing him or her to continue in the abuse. Turn the abuser into the authorities if he or she won't repent.

9. *Turn the vengeance over to God and over to God's human authorities* (see Rom. 12:19-20; 13:1). Let God do the disciplining in your marriage. Never try to take His place. Never protect anyone, even a family member, from legitimate church discipline or from impartial civil justice. These authorities are instituted by God for your protection and for the sake of social justice.

10. *Replace the old resentful feelings with the forgiving love of Christ* (see Matt. 12:43-45; Eph. 4:31-32). A spiritual vacuum is dangerous. Anything not controlled by the Holy Spirit will soon attract evil spirits (see Matt. 12:43-45). The result of forgiveness should never be emptiness or defeat, but rather actions of overflowing love.

What You Do Not Have to Do

1. *You do not have to feel good about the person who hurt you—either before or after you forgive.* Forgiveness is an issue between you and God. It does not put a stamp of approval on another's behavior. It does not automatically rebuild trust. It does not make you like someone who has hurt you. It simply releases the offense and lets you focus on the problem, not the problem-producer.

2. *You don't have to tell the other person about your resentful feelings unless Scripture or the Holy Spirit tells you to do so* (see Matt. 5:23-26; 18:15-17). The need to forgive is between you and God; the need to ask for forgiveness is between you and another person. If the issue is a need for reconciliation between two estranged people, both of whom are aware of the tension, then go make peace. But if the other person is not aware of it, or it's no big deal to that person, then keep your personal forgiveness between you and God. Every Christian should follow the guidance of the Holy Spirit.

3. *You don't have to wait until you are ready to forgive.* You can obey God's Word right now.

Painful Memories

Unless your marriage is still in its earliest stages, you are sure to have some painful memories. The way to deal with these hurtful times with your spouse is to forgive. We will explain how to do this as a couple in chapter 12, where we present the Steps to Setting Your Marriage Free.

We start this process of forgiveness by recalling good memories. During times of estrangement, all a couple can think about is the bad times. It is always helpful to keep life in perspective. Every couple has had some good times, and most spouses are doing the best they can. Forgiveness is the key to an enduring marriage.

In conclusion, consider the following story from a woman who, after more than 50 years of secrecy, shared the following private story with "Dear Abby":

I was 20 and he was 26. We had been married two years and I hadn't dreamed he could be unfaithful. The awful truth was brought home to me when a young widow from a neighboring farm came to tell me she was carrying my husband's child. My world collapsed. I wanted to die. I fought an urge to kill her—and him.

I knew that wasn't the answer. I prayed for strength and guidance. And it came. I knew I had to forgive this man, and I did. I forgave her, too. I calmly told my husband what I had learned and the three of us worked out a solution together. (What a frightened little creature she was!) The baby was born in my home. Everyone thought I had given birth and that my neighbor was "helping me." Actually it was the other way around. But the widow was spared humiliation (she had three other children), and the little boy was raised as my own. He never knew the truth.

Was this divine compensation for my own inability to bear a child? I do not know. I have never mentioned this incident to my husband. It has been a closed chapter in our lives for 50 years. But I've read the love and gratitude in his eyes a thousand times.[2]

Notes
1. Barbara Dafoe Whitehead, "Dan Quayle Was Right," *The Atlantic Monthly*, vol. 271, no. 4 (April 1993), p. 47.
2. J. Allan Petersen, *The Myth of the Greener Grass* (Wheaton, IL: Tyndale House Publishers, Inc., 1983), pp. 146-147.

Group Discussion

1. How can seeing your role as primarily that of parent be unhealthy for both your children and your marriage?

2. Why do we need to forgive—and forgive again?

3. How would you define the ministry of reconciliation?

4. Why do you need to forgive your spouse even if he or she doesn't ask for it or won't repent?

5. What is forgiveness?

6. How do you forgive from your heart?

Devotional Guide for Couples

Read Psalm 32 with the knowledge that David wrote this after he had sinned with Bathsheba and discuss why it is so important to walk in the light and speak the truth in love.

WHEN ONLY ONE WILL TRY

To the married I give this command (not I, but the Lord): A wife must not separate from her husband. But if she does, she must remain unmarried or else be reconciled to her husband. And a husband must not divorce his wife.

1 Corinthians 7:10-11

H ave you ever felt like giving in to despair? You've given so much, tried so hard, and your marriage partner still does not seem interested. He or she may be a workaholic, alcoholic or sexaholic. Maybe he won't talk. Maybe she won't make love. Maybe he's abusive. Maybe she spends all the money. Or maybe your spouse is responsible but boring, satisfied with this marriage that leaves you unsatisfied. Does God have answers when only one mate will try? I believe He does.

Doris saw her life with Drake go from bad to worse. Both of them were raised in Christian families, but they knew nothing about Christ's freedom. They were content as Christians, financially secure and pleased with their three grown girls. They were reasonably happy and thought they had a good marriage. Doris, however, had this nagging sense that something was missing.

Drake made a major financial investment that turned into a disaster. Stress hit big time, and for the first time in his life he began to experience panic attacks. His financial stability was going down the drain and the panic attacks persisted. To make matters worse, Doris collapsed while visiting her daughters in another state. She was rushed to the hospital for emergency surgery and could not travel, even to return home, for four months. When she did return home, their marriage did not improve. In Doris's own words:

> It seemed like all the things on which we had based our value were in jeopardy. Our life appeared to be collapsing before our

eyes and we were helpless. Our marriage, which we thought to be so strong, was in serious difficulty. We had never experienced real depression before, but now there seemed to be no respite from it. We didn't understand. We were Christians who had always tried to do the "right thing." We felt powerless. Satan also uses circumstances to his own end and he was relentless in his attack. We felt increasingly unhappy.[1]

Along with a close friend, the wife of a former pastor (whose marriage was also in trouble), Doris attended one of Neil's seminars. She found her freedom in Christ and reaffirmed her identity as a child of God. Christ's freedom in her innermost *being* changed her attitude about outward living. Because she was free on the inside, she gained Christ's confidence on the outside. Life was looking up, except for one thing—Drake's attitude. He was pleased that she was encouraged by the conference, but he felt no need to attend one himself.

Doris played him a video from the conference series,[2] but he only went to sleep. She tried to get him to read *The Bondage Breaker*. No luck. She even made arrangements with her friend, the former pastor's wife, for the two couples to watch one of Neil's videos together. *Both husbands* went to sleep! What's a wife to do when her husband won't even try? Doris must have been praying, however, because when she reached her wit's end, God took over.

Drake's father, who had been battling cancer, entered the final days of his fight with the dreaded disease. On the flight to visit him, Drake began to read a copy of *The Bondage Breaker* that Doris had brought along for a mutual friend. He was so impressed with the book that he began to tell Doris how good it was. Shock!

On arrival, the couple found Drake's father weak but alert. When Drake told his father about the book, he wanted to hear it. This godly man had been a fine Christian for years, so Drake and Doris took turns reading the book to him. He loved it!

With tears streaming down his cheeks, Drake's dad shared how he had needed to hear these truths. Even on his deathbed, Satan was accusing him! He went home to be with the Lord, free in Christ. Needless to say, Drake found his freedom, too. The panic attacks disappeared. In time, the Lord restored their marriage and their finances. Best of all, God transformed their relationship with the Lord Jesus. They moved from performance-based Christianity to freedom in Christ.

What happened to Doris's friend, the wife of the former pastor? She and her husband separated for six weeks until his pride was broken. He then became willing to read *The Bondage Breaker* and take its message to heart. Both he and his wife used their new sense of *being* free in Christ as a basis for *doing* work on their marriage. Drake and Doris eventually had the privilege of standing up with the former pastor and his wife in a precious time of renewing their marriage vows.

Separate *Doing* from *Being*

Separating *doing* from *being* has been the theme of this book. There are many Christian books and speakers giving good advice about what to do. A subtle form of Christian behaviorism results from an overemphasis on doing: do better, try harder, give more, follow this advice. Many of us try and try, and fail and fail, until we finally give up. Something sinister, something weird, something demonic fouls up our best efforts. Our marriages end in divorce, and our children suffer.

The problem is that we try to change what we *do* without letting Christ change who we *are*. In order for our marriages to work, we need the life of Christ, not just the words of Christ. Christianity is not a good idea; it is a new life in Christ. Christianity is not an act; it is a life. We have no natural ability to change who we are, but Christ does. Successful living is always characterized by character before career, maturity before ministry and being before doing.

The same goes for successful marriages. Health problems escalate when marriages fail. A report by the National Institute for Healthcare Research shows a significant link between divorce and early death, drug and alcohol use, and various health problems. One discovery found that divorced men face the same risk for cancer as a man who smokes a pack of cigarettes a day. Susan Larson, who coauthored the report, said, "Early death from both cardiovascular disease and strokes doubled for divorced men compared to married men."[3]

Too many people, including evangelical Christians, consider divorce an option. They rationalize the Bible's truth that God hates divorce (see Mal. 2:13-16; Mark 10:2-12; 1 Cor. 7:10-14) and focus only on the exception clauses (see Matt. 5:31-32; 1 Cor. 7:15). Newspaper columnist Mona Charen explains why so few speak out against this tragic blight on our society:

Divorce is such an accepted part of the national landscape that even cultural crusaders have sometimes held their fire. To condemn divorce is to rebuke not just strangers but your sister, your cousins, your best friend and yourself. The wreckage divorce has created in the lives of children is too massive to be denied.[4]

What is this massive evidence? In *The Atlantic Monthly*, Barbara Dafoe Whitehead shares some disturbing facts:

According to a growing body of social-scientific evidence, children in families disrupted by divorce and out-of-wedlock birth do worse than children in intact families on several measures of well-being. Children in single-parent families are six times as likely to be poor. They are also likely to stay poor longer. Twenty-two percent of children in one-parent families will experience poverty during childhood for seven years or more, as compared with only two percent of children in two-parent families. A 1988 survey by the National Center for Health Statistics found that children in single-parent families are two to three times as likely as children in two-parent families to have emotional and behavioral problems. They are also more likely to drop out of high school, to get pregnant as teenagers, to abuse drugs and to be in trouble with the law. Compared with children in intact families, children from disrupted families are at a much higher risk for physical or sexual abuse.

Contrary to popular belief, many children do not "bounce back" after divorce or remarriage. Difficulties that are associated with family breakup often persist into adulthood. Children who grow up in single-parent or stepparent families are less successful as adults, particularly in the two domains of life—love and work—that are most essential to happiness. Needless to say, not all children experience such negative effects. However, research shows that many children from disrupted families have a harder time achieving intimacy in a relationship, forming a stable marriage or even holding a steady job.[5]

Time magazine reported the following:

"Almost half of children of divorces enter adulthood as worried, under-achieving, self-deprecating and sometimes angry young men and women," reports Judith Wallerstein, director of the Center for the Family in Transition and author of *Second Chance* (Ticknor and Fields, 1988). Her conclusion is drawn from interviews conducted over a 15-year period with 60 families, mostly white middle class. It included 131 children, who were 2 to 18 years old at the time of the divorce. Other Wallerstein findings:

- Three out of five youngsters felt rejected by at least one parent.
- Half grew up in settings in which the parents were warring with each other even after the divorce.
- Two-thirds of the girls, many of whom had seemingly sailed through the crisis, suddenly became deeply anxious as young adults, unable to make lasting commitments and fearful of betrayal in intimate relationships.
- Many boys, who were overly troubled in the postdivorce years, failed to develop a sense of independence, confidence or purpose. They drifted in and out of college and from job to job.[6]

The traditional wisdom that it's worth saving a marriage or staying with a bad one for the sake of the children seems wiser than ever before. Moving a marriage from divorce to freedom may seem hard, but in the long run it is easier than living with a broken marriage and family.

Yet it takes more than trying harder, more than good techniques, and more than advanced relationship skills to save a troubled marriage. It takes sacrifice, dedication, commitment. It takes putting our hands into the hand of the Holy Spirit and allowing Him to lead us in the light of God's Word, even to the Cross. It takes adjusting our lives to God's ways and believing His truth.

Not Divorce, but Freedom

Often, only one person in a marriage will be willing to go through the Steps to Setting Your Marriage Free. The good news is that most of the spiritual bondage in the marriage can be broken by one Christian spouse. God hears and answers prayer, even if it's only one person who prays.

So why not try it? After all, what's the worst thing that could happen? By believing and repenting, you will become a better person. You may even save the marriage without a word being spoken. Is this not similar to what Peter counseled Christian wives with unbelieving husbands? "Your beauty . . . should be that of your inner self, the unfading beauty of a gentle and quiet spirit, which is of great worth in God's sight" (1 Pet. 3:3-4). Your spouse may be "won over without words" (v. 1) by your behavior.

With this in mind, we have adapted the Steps to Setting Your Marriage Free for the one spouse who is willing to try. You can download those Steps from Neil's website at www.discipleshipcounselingmin istries.org or www.ficm.org. If you really want to experience your freedom, begin with the personal Steps to Freedom in Christ. If you find difficulty at any point, ask a trusted pastor or Christian prayer partner to lead you through them. Then work through the marriage steps by seeking Christ's cleansing of your marriage relationship. However, remember that even after processing the "Marriage Steps for One Spouse," a long and difficult road may yet lie ahead.

After only two years of marriage, Lance (an unbeliever) and Wendy (a halfhearted believer) were living like married singles. He was deeply involved in sports, and she was busy at work. Wendy was not getting the attention she needed, so she began to look for it at work. It didn't take long to find an attentive male—and an adulterous affair.

Lance was so busy between work and sports that it was easy for Wendy to hide her time away with her illicit lover. She played the role of a faithful wife, and Lance suspected nothing. Then one night when she did not come home, a red flag started waving in Lance's mind.

Lance confronted Wendy, and soon her double life was out in the open. Now they could deal with the problems in their marriage, but instead of resolving anything, they fought. Wendy left home for the other man. Lance was deeply upset and spent a lot of time crying—although he was not normally a crier by nature. The days of separation turned into weeks, and the weeks turned into months. After five months, Wendy filed for divorce, which in time became final.

Although he was now divorced, Lance did not give up. He turned to the Church and received Christ as His Lord and Savior. He wanted Wendy back, so he decided to go to work on himself. He pursued Christ with a passion, making every possible change for the better. Near the end of 10 months of separation, Wendy, seeing the changes in Lance, rededicated her life to Christ. Once Jesus was again allowed His rightful place, she became intensely uncomfortable with her adultery and, although divorced, returned home to Lance.

The two forgave each other—for neglect and for adultery—and opened a new chapter in their lives. They agreed to close the book on their past sins and look ahead to their new life in Christ. They remarried. It's now years later, and Lance and Wendy have helped many other couples find hope when everything has seemed hopeless.

"I learned to forgive Wendy," Lance said. "Even years later it still hurts, but I have learned to forgive."

Living with Pain

If you are the only one who will try in your marriage, and if the marriage is deeply flawed, then you may be living with constant pain. During such a time, turn to the Psalms. Many were written in times of pain as the psalmist cried out to God for help against his enemies. The Psalms help us during our times of trouble:

I am in pain and distress; may your salvation, O God, protect me (Ps. 69:29).

He heals the brokenhearted and binds up their wounds (Ps. 147:3).

Keep me safe, O God, for in you I take refuge (Ps. 16:1).

How can you as a faithful Christian spouse live with the pain of a broken marriage? How do you tolerate the spouse who keeps on hurting you again and again? How can you be responsible without becoming a sick controller or a codependent? What if your spouse is an addict, a thief, an adulterer or a credit card junkie? In Chuck's book *Running the Red Lights* (Regal Books), he wrote the following about being responsible or irresponsible:

- I will *let* you be responsible. And I will not knowingly contribute to your being irresponsible.
- I will not try to force you to be responsible by nagging, condemning, scolding, moralizing.
- I will not knowingly let you be irresponsible by removing the consequences when you do what is wrong.
- I will stand by you, care for you, cry with you; but I will not bail you out time after time after time.
- I will not personally judge you, pretending I am your judge instead of God.
- Neither will I personally provide a shelter for your sin, pretending I am your Savior instead of Christ.
- I will love you, accept you, forgive you and give you a fresh start whenever you ask for it.[7]

If you begin to put these principles into practice, your pain may increase—at least at first. Sometimes, things have to get worse before they get better. Never forget that Jesus lived with pain. The prophet Isaiah predicted the suffering of the Messiah: "He was despised and rejected by men, a man of sorrows, and familiar with suffering" (53:3). Hebrews tells us, "Although he was a son, he learned obedience from what he suffered" (Heb. 5:8). Jesus said to His disciples, "You are those who have stood by me in my trials" (Luke 22:28). When no one else understands your pain, Jesus does.

How did Jesus treat those who mistreated Him? How did He treat Judas Iscariot, one of the Twelve, who betrayed Him? The Bible reveals that although He warned Judas, He also protected him from the anger of the disciples. He appealed to Judas to change but also treated him as a friend until the moment of betrayal. He was neither deceived nor fooled by Judas's hypocrisy. But neither did Jesus use His knowledge against Judas to do him in.

Jesus suffered for the sins of the whole world, but His crucifixion came directly from Judas' treachery. Instead of attacking Judas, exposing him or even protecting Himself, Jesus considered Judas's evil acts as part of the Father's perfect plan for His life. Yet Jesus did not allow Judas to sway Him from God's best, nor did He pay attention to Judas's criticism (see John 12:4-8). What a model for us on how to treat the one who betrays us, even if it's a spouse!

Having Wisdom

When only one spouse will try, God's wisdom is needed. Pray for wisdom, seek wisdom, live in wisdom. Sometimes we develop the most character and gain the wisest insights in the worst of relationships. One of the great Bible promises for wisdom links it with trouble and trials. With your marriage in mind, read Eugene Peterson's paraphrase of this promise found in James 1:2-8:

> Consider it a sheer gift, friends, when tests and challenges come at you from all sides. You know that under pressure, your faith-life is forced into the open and shows its true colors. So don't try to get out of anything prematurely. Let it do its work so you become mature and well-developed, not deficient in any way.
>
> If you don't know what you're doing, pray to the Father. He loves to help. You'll get his help, and won't be condescended to

when you ask for it. Ask boldly, believingly, without a second thought. People who "worry their prayers" are like wind-whipped waves. Don't think you're going to get anything from the Master that way, adrift at sea, keeping all your options open (*THE MESSAGE*).

Spiritual wisdom is the bridge between being and doing. Wisdom is knowing who we are in Christ and who God is and then applying that spiritual union of God and humanity to real-life situations. Seeing life from God's perspective—accompanied by His presence—brings new life and perspective to our marriages.

So far, our focus in this chapter has been on becoming the kind of person who can save or improve a marriage. From this point on, our focus will now be on doing. Recall the analogy of a hub and spokes at the beginning of this book. We first make sure we are connected to Christ, our hub, and then the spokes give us direction to responsible behavior.

Hidden Creativity

What if you could become more creative in your marriage? What if the Holy Spirit would lead you to the very thoughts, words and acts that would put your marriage back together, healthy and whole? Would you adjust your life to His leading? Would you determine to become, by God's grace, the best possible marriage partner He created you to be? If your answers are yes, we have good news for you.

All who have received Christ and live in Him are united with His creativity. We share in the "fullness" of God, which is our inheritance in Christ. Notice what Colossians says about God's fullness in Christ: "For in Christ all the *fullness* of the Deity lives in bodily form, and you have been given *fullness* in Christ" (Col. 2:9-10, emphasis added).

The first half of the verse makes sense to those who understand that Christ is God the Son, the second Person of the Trinity. All the fullness of God lives in the resurrected, risen and reigning Lord Jesus. Because Christ lives in us and He has all the fullness of God, it follows that the fullness of God lives in us, too. We are crucified, buried, made alive, raised up and seated with Christ at the right hand of God (see Rom. 6:3-5; Gal. 2:20; Eph. 2:4-6; Col. 3:1-3). Because we are united with Christ (see Phil. 2:1), His fullness lives in us. That does not make us God, but it does mean that God Himself *and His character qualities* live within us. We have become a partaker of the Divine Nature (see 2 Pet. 1:4).

We can't exhaust all the meaning of the fullness of Christ within us, but one thing is obvious from the context: It includes His authority and His creativity (see Col. 1:16; 2:9-10). As *THE MESSAGE* puts it in Colossians 2:9, "You don't need a telescope, a microscope, or a horoscope to realize the fullness of Christ." We are united with Christ, so in Him we have spiritual authority to do His will as well as the creativity to live it, if we abide in Him. This Spirit-empowered creativity shows up when:

- Christ gives us an idea that works in our marriage
- Christ inspires a thought that is helpful to our spouse
- Christ puts the right words in our mouth (maybe with our children or grandchildren) just when we need them
- Christ enables us to show we care, which is greatly appreciated
- Christ does something fresh and new through us that we had not done or thought of before

Christ's creative leading becomes evident when we are filled with His Spirit. It may come in unexpected moments in troubled marriages, so we need to look for it, pray for it, expect it. When it comes, we should respond in faith and acknowledge Christ as the source. That is how we glorify God in our bodies—by manifesting His presence in the world.

Spontaneous creativity is a cherished part of being united with Christ. Not only does He make us creative—Christ Himself is also creative in re-creating us (see Phil. 1:6; 2:12-13). No matter how bad a marriage is, Christ can fulfill the deepest longings of both spouses. His creativity is at work within us to fulfill all of His promises. He never promises us a great marriage, but He does promise His fullness, including His authority in prayer and His creativity in our actions.

Janice and Ted

Janice, 26, had two children, and her husband, Ted, was committing adultery. Each night, Ted came home for dinner and then went to his girlfriend's house where he slept until morning. Janice was desperate and turned to a biblical counselor for help.

The counselor asked Janice if she was willing to fight for her marriage. She assured him that she was willing to do anything. Sensing her eagerness and Christian attitude, he gave her a tough assignment. He recommended that she treat her husband just like she would treat Jesus. He challenged her to love and serve him, even for the short time he was home, just the way she would care for Jesus if He were visiting her home.

Janice reminded the counselor that Ted was nothing like Jesus. He was sleeping with another woman and doing nothing to build their marriage. The counselor outlined her options: continue what she had been doing (which was making her miserable), yell and scream and threaten, divorce him, or take the biblical approach and let her actions match her prayers. Assured that Janice was praying for Ted, the counselor again asked her to love and serve Ted for one week, just as if he were Jesus. She agreed to try.

Janice dressed her best each night, fixed Ted's favorite meal, put the paper beside his favorite chair and did everything she could think of to treat him as if he were Jesus Himself. The first night, Ted muttered under his breath and left as usual. The second night, he said a few civil words to Janice and then left for his girlfriend's house. The third night, he asked Janice what was going on. She explained she was treating him the way she always should have. That night, he did not go to his girlfriend's but slept in a separate bedroom at home. By the end of the week, he was seeing his girlfriend less often and staying in the house more often.

When Janice returned to talk with the counselor, she knew, for the first time in many months, she had Ted's attention. The counselor suggested that when the timing was right, she share with Ted that a man at church was teaching her how to treat her husband and that this man wanted to meet Ted, too. The moment came, and Ted agreed to talk with the man whose input had so dramatically altered his wife's attitudes and actions.

In talking with the counselor, Ted openly admitted he was "messing around" with another woman. The counselor asked how the relationship was going. Ted indicated that although they had a sexual relationship, he really didn't love her. She was putting a lot of pressure on him to leave Janice and marry her. However, he was thinking about breaking off the affair and trying to work things out with Janice.

By the time the session was over, Ted had not only committed to coming home, but he had also received Christ as his Lord and Savior. The counselor led both Ted and Janice through a time of repenting before God and forgiving each other. (This is one of the purposes of the "Steps to Setting Your Marriage Free" that we discuss in the next chapter.)

Janice and Ted met with the counselor for many months on a weekly basis. Some sessions were helpful, while others were painful. But they kept growing in Christ and remained faithful in their new attitudes toward one another. They both became active in the church, growing in Christ and maturing in their marriage. Not all stories turn out as well as this one, but many do.[8]

Remove Excuses

When only one spouse will try, a good strategy is to remove the other spouse's excuses. Wayward husbands and wives most often feel the need to justify their actions. Often they will engage in blame-shifting. They will say things such as, "Well, you always . . ." "You never . . ." "What about the time that you . . ." "You're not so perfect either, because you . . ." "It's hopeless, because you . . ."

If you are alert, you can begin compiling this list of excuses and begin to remove them. The process of removing the excuses will build your character and improve conditions in the marriage. Surprisingly, the marriage partner who is not trying usually is neither pleased nor impressed with this change. A second list of new excuses most often emerges. It's good to know this ahead of time so that you will not be surprised and give up hope. A new set of excuses is normal.

Simply begin removing the second list—and then expect a third. By the time the third set of excuses is removed, there will almost always be a visible change in the indifferent partner's behavior. Once in awhile it's for the worse, but most often it's for the better. Meanwhile, concentrate on meeting your spouse's needs (and keep meeting them). Become an expert in speaking your spouse's love language. Get really good at it!

Winning Through Losing

Jesus taught an interesting principle about losing in order to win: "For whoever wants to save his life will lose it, but whoever loses his life for me will save it" (Luke 9:24). This principle applies to a hurting marriage. The person who loses a natural life by following Jesus' teaching and example in a troubled marriage wins real life in Christ.

The world system says, "Don't put up with that garbage. You have rights, too. I know this single person who is really lonely. Let me introduce you." Your friends will say, "Get out. Haven't you had enough? Here's the name of a good divorce attorney." However, Jesus teaches us to love our enemies, stand by our marriages and sacrifice ourselves in love. It's not easy, but often it's effective. If you are free in Christ, living in the Spirit and *supported by a group of caring Christian people,* you will become a better person—and you might save your marriage. Don't miss the support of other Christians committed to saving marriages; their encouragement and prayers are essential to your success.

Never confuse winning through losing—what the Bible calls "humility"—with becoming a doormat or a pushover. The one who finds freedom in Christ becomes stronger in the Lord, not weaker. The humble spouse, the one who is committed to winning by losing, also learns to communicate feelings, desires and requests in a compelling way.

When Christ is energizing you and His creativity is at work within you, you can count on His help. He will help you *win* through losing, not lose through winning. He will help you attain your true goal of becoming a man or woman of God. He may rescue your marriage as well.

Making an Appeal

A painful marriage always sends the faithful spouse to prayer. Prayer, sometimes coupled with fasting, leads to new insight and fresh power. Prayer leads to God's plan of action. If the plan is big enough to call for a change in your role or the marriage relationship, it will require an appeal to your spouse. An appeal is a call for a change, for help or for a specific request to be granted. A good appeal communicates something intensely desired in a way most likely to be heard.

Watch for just the right moment to speak up. Appeals made in the heat of anger or with the cutting sarcasm of a critical spirit seldom carry much weight. If necessary, make an appointment or create the right time to share the burden of your heart. When the right moment comes, breathe a quick prayer and seize the opportunity. The grave danger is in backing off when you should move ahead. Tact and sensitivity will help. So will healthy eye contact, warm nonverbal signals, kind words, carefully worded phrases and good questions.

When you make the appeal, let your loyalty show. Express appreciation for anything positive the uncaring spouse may have done. Clearly show your respect for your spouse's position, as well as an acknowledgment for any sensitivity or support he or she has ever shown you. A rebellious spirit always wounds and never heals. With tact and sensitivity, tell your story and share your feelings, including the desired change God has laid on your heart. If possible, tie your appeal to your spouse's interests and desires. Ask yourself, *How does this plan, idea or feeling tie in with my spouse's best intentions?*

Make a clear, polite request for what you would like. If your spouse agrees to your request, take action at the proper time. If it is denied, don't argue. In a cheery voice, respond with, "That's okay" or "No problem." If it's something really serious and the denial is a major blow, respond calmly, "I'm sorry you feel that way, but you have a right to your own opinion." Then, when you are alone, pray and ask yourself some important questions: *Why was my appeal denied? Was it loyal, tactful, clear? Had I earned the right to be heard? Did I speak in a good spirit and with God's timing? Is this answer God's message to me? Should I accept it or regroup and look for the right chance to make a new appeal? What does God want me to do next?*

To make a good appeal, always remember the following:

1. Know your limitations. Only God can change your spouse.
2. Prepare your plan. Think it through in prayer.
3. Appeal with feeling. Keep courtesy and respect in the forefront.
4. Follow through with your plan. Obeying God is more important than pleasing people.

A godly appeal can touch a human spirit and change a convinced mind. Persist in making heartfelt appeals for specific changes. Space these appeals at least two or more months apart. Each time, pray hard, look for the right moment, and follow the Holy Spirit's guidance. Remember, it took a long time to develop the problems you face and it may take what seems like forever to resolve them. Never give up—never! God delights in doing what seems impossible to us.

Protected

When your marriage is in trouble and you are the only one who is willing to try to correct the problems, put on the full armor of God (see Eph. 6:10-20). Take your stand against the devil's schemes as he attempts to lead you astray and destroy your marriage.

Put on the belt of truth and make honesty and integrity your way of life. Never tell lies. This enables you to stand against the father of lies. Wear the breastplate of righteousness. Standing in Christ's righteousness is your defense against Satan's accusations. Lift the shield of faith, which stops the enemy's temptations and accusations. Put on the helmet of salvation, the full deliverance from sin and from lasting damage to your mind. Grasp the sword of the Spirit, the spoken Word of God that gives you just the right words at the time you most need them. Buckle on the boots of peace, always ready to move into spiritual battle as a peacemaker. Let peace flow from your identity in Christ, your forgiveness, your repentance and your freedom. Then pray in the Spirit as He leads (see Neil's book *Praying by the Power of the Holy Spirit* [Harvest House]).

You can achieve your goal to become a godly man or a godly woman. Be God's instrument to restore and rebuild your marriage. If you do, three or four generations to come will thank you. When you stand before the judgment seat of Christ, Jesus will praise you (see 2 Cor. 5:10).

Notes

1. From a personal letter mailed to Neil Anderson.
2. Dr. Neil T. Anderson, *Resolving Personal Conflicts* and *Resolving Spiritual Conflicts* (Ventura, CA: Gospel Light, 1992). They can be purchased at Christian bookstores or from Freedom in Christ Ministries (sales@ficm.org).
3. Dan Davidson, ed., *The Pastor's Weekly Briefing*, vol. 3, no. 36 (September 8, 1995), p. 2. Pastoral Ministries, Focus on the Family, Colorado Springs, CO 80995.
4. Mona Charen, "We Can't Separate Divorce and Social Chaos," *The Orange County Register*, Monday, June 19, 1995, Metro section, p. 7.
5. Barbara Dafoe Whitehead, "Dan Quayle Was Right," *The Atlantic Monthly*, vol. 271, no. 4 (April 1993), p. 47.
6. Anastasia Toufexis, quoted in Georgia Harbison/New York, "The Lasting Wounds of Divorce," *Time* magazine, vol. 133, no. 6 (February 6, 1989), p. 61.
7. Charles Mylander, *Running the Red Lights, Putting the Brakes on Sexual Temptation* (Ventura, CA: Regal Books, 1986), pp. 215-216.
8. Jimmy Evans, *Marriage on the Rock* (New York: McCracken Press, 1994), pp. 203-212.

Group Discussion

1. What are some good and bad ideas on how to motivate your spouse to work together with you for a better marriage?

2. Why is who we are more important than what we do?

3. What can a spouse do for the marriage when the other person remains indifferent?

4. What are some creative ways to make your marriage better?

5. How can you appeal to a resistant spouse?

Devotional Guide for Couples

Read Luke 6:20-38 and discuss how we are to relate to others according to Jesus.

STEPS TO SETTING YOUR MARRIAGE FREE

This final chapter presents the process for setting your marriage free. Our intention here is not to help you manage your conflicts; rather, we believe your conflicts can be resolved in Christ through genuine repentance and faith in Him. The Lord will be your wonderful counselor and the Holy Spirit will guide you into all truth. That truth will set you free. If you have a relatively mature marriage relationship that is characterized by mutual trust and respect, you can work through this process without outside assistance. We have taken the time to do so with our wives.

We can't encourage you strongly enough to first work through the personal Steps to Freedom in Christ. If both partners have dealt with their own issues, they are then ready to deal with their marital issues. Set aside an evening when you can be alone and choose a location where you wouldn't be embarrassed to read and process the Steps out loud. If you cannot get through the Steps on your own, call someone who has been trained to help others. The personal Steps are available from the Freedom in Christ Ministries office or from your local bookstore.

As we mentioned in the prior chapter, if your spouse is unwilling to participate, you can obtain a modification of these marriage Steps from Neil's website at ficm.org or www.discipleshipcounselingmin istries.org. These Steps have been developed for those who desire to be totally honest and responsible before God, even though their spouse is not willing to process the Steps. There are also "Steps to Beginning Your Marriage Free," which can be used for premarital counseling. You can also order a free copy of these Steps at the same website.

Are you willing to be honest with God and each other? Are you willing to allow God to show you anything He desires? If so, share your intentions with each other before you begin. God's will is to reveal blockages in intimacy within your marriage and to make your marriage even better. He wants the life of Christ to display His glory in you and your marriage.

You must both agree to assume personal responsibility for your own issues and not attack the other person's character or family. Allow the Holy Spirit to bring guidance and conviction to you and your spouse. Do not try to play the role of the Holy Spirit in your spouse's life. This process will not work unless you speak the truth in love, walk in the light and assume responsibility for your own attitudes and actions. The Lord loves you and wants to see you free from your past, be alive in Him, and committed to one another. If your relationship is experiencing difficulty, we suggest you have a responsible person assist you. It would be best to have a person whom you both can trust.

Tips for Groups

If you have completed the first 11 chapters of this book in your small-group or Sunday School class and desire to complete the Steps at a weekend retreat, we suggest that you and your group spend Friday evening in corporate prayer and fellowship. If you have not worked through the individual Steps to Freedom in Christ, then Friday night would be the time to do so. The accommodations must allow privacy for each couple.

In a group setting, each Step should begin with instruction by the facilitator, followed by the group praying the prayer that begins each section. Each couple should then finish the Step together in a private location. We have conducted a Setting Your Marriage Free Conference with the above schedule at hotels and churches.

If you intend to use these Steps in your church, we strongly suggest that you use this book or cover the same material in your preaching and teaching before you attempt to go through the process. Members of Sunday School classes, discipleship groups and small-group ministries that are reading this book can process these Steps in their weekly scheduled meetings. You can go through one Step per week. Each Step would be completed by every couple in their own home on their own.

We prefer that you first work through the material taught in *Victory Over the Darkness* (Regal Books) and *The Bondage Breaker* (Harvest House). This can be done by using the small-group curriculum entitled *Beta, The Next Step in Discipleship* (Regal Books). If you wish to start a Christ-centered discipleship counseling ministry in your church to help individuals and marriages, see the appendix.

Are you ready to begin? If so, start the process by praying the following prayer together:

Prayer of Commitment by Husband and Wife

Dear heavenly Father,

We love You and we thank You for Your grace, truth, love, power, forgiveness and blessings in Christ. We can love each other because You first loved us. We can forgive because we have been forgiven, and we can accept one another just as You have accepted us. We desire nothing more than to know and do Your will. We ask for Your divine guidance and protection during this time of seeking freedom in our marriage. We give ourselves emotionally to You and each other and ask You to free us so that we can share from our hearts.

We buckle on the belt of Your truth, put on the breastplate of Your righteousness and commit ourselves to the gospel of peace. We hold up the shield of faith and stand against the flaming arrows of the enemy. We commit ourselves to take every thought captive in obedience to You. We put on the helmet of salvation, which assures us of Your forgiveness, Your life and our freedom in You. We put off the old self and put on the new self that is being renewed in Your image. We take the sword of the Spirit, the spoken Word of God, to defend ourselves against the father of lies. We acknowledge our dependence on You and understand that apart from You we can do nothing.

We pray that You will grant us genuine repentance and living faith. We desire our marriage to become a beautiful picture of Your relationship with us. We ask You to fill us with Your Holy Spirit, lead us into all truth and set us free in Christ.

In Jesus' precious name, we pray. Amen.

Have a Bible close at hand as well as a pad of paper to record the issues you are seeking to resolve. However, before you proceed through the Steps, you first need to complete one small but important exercise to get you started. To resolve conflicts, you must look at all the problems, which can be quite negative. So take the time to answer the following two questions:

1. What five character qualities do you most appreciate about your spouse?

2. What five things does your spouse do that you really appreciate?

Write these answers on your pad of paper, and then share your responses with your spouse. You are now ready to begin working through the Steps to Setting Your Marriage Free.

Step One:
Establish God's Priority for Marriage

The first Step is to seek the Lord's wisdom concerning how completely you have left your father and mother and have bonded to one another.

Remember the words of Jesus: "He who loves father or mother more than Me is not worthy of Me; and he who loves son or daughter more than Me is not worthy of Me" (Matt. 10:37, *NASB*). This does not mean you don't honor your father and mother, but it does mean you can have only one Lord in your life. It means your spiritual heritage must take precedence over your natural heritage.

In what ways could you be holding on to some unhealthy ties that are keeping you from committing yourself fully to the Lord and to each other? Those ties might be physical, emotional, spiritual or financial. Ask the Lord to reveal to your mind the ways you have not left father and mother and failed to cleave only to one another.

> *Dear heavenly Father,*
>
> *We humbly submit ourselves to You and ask for Your divine guidance. We ask that You reveal to our minds any way that we have allowed our physical heritage to be more important than our spiritual heritage. Show us anything in our lives that has taken on a greater sense of importance to us than our relationship to You. We also ask You to show us in what ways we have not honorably left our mothers and our fathers physically, spiritually, mentally, emotionally or financially. We desire to be spiritually bonded to You in order that we can be fully bonded to each other.*
>
> *In Jesus' name, we pray. Amen.*

Both you and your spouse should sit silently before the Lord to individually and honestly consider your relationship with God and with your own parents. Do not consider your spouse's relationship with your mother-in-law and father-in-law. Let the Lord be the judge, and allow your spouse to assume responsibility for his or her parents. Now, each one of you should consider these questions:

1. Does the approval of relatives mean more to me than the approval of God?
2. Am I still trying to live up to the expectations of my relatives?
3. Is my relationship with God the most important relationship in my life?
4. Is my relationship with my spouse the second most important relationship in my life?
5. Would I be willing to sever any other relationship that would threaten my relationship with God and my spouse, even if that meant separating myself from members of my natural family?

Leaving father and mother cannot mean dishonoring them. Being disrespectful to your parents cannot lead to freedom. Consider these questions:

1. Have you gone against your parents' counsel in getting married?
2. If so, have you prayerfully tried to reconcile your differences and receive their blessing?
3. In what ways have you been disrespectful of your parents or not shown appreciation for what they have done?

> **Note**: If you feel your parents have wronged you, you will be given an opportunity to forgive them later in the Steps.

Now write down any ungodly way you are still bonded to your own parents or stepparents

1. Physically
2. Spiritually
3. Mentally
4. Emotionally
5. Financially

When you have both finished your lists, privately confess it to God. Then share with each other what you have learned. If your past ties to your family have affected your relationship with each other in a negative way, ask each other for forgiveness. If you have been unduly critical of your in-laws, ask your spouse to forgive you.

Conclude this Step with the following prayer together:

Dear heavenly Father,

We thank You for revealing these important issues to us. We rededicate our lives to You and to each other. Our desire is to become one flesh and one spirit in Christ. May Your Holy Spirit bond us together in love for You and for each other. Show us how we can rightly relate to our earthly parents and other relatives. We confess any way that we have dishonored our parents and ask You to show us how we can honor them according to Your will. Thank You for Your forgiveness.

In Jesus' precious name, we pray. Amen.

Note for those who previously have been married:
You may want to ask the Lord if any unhealthy bond remains between you and your ex-spouse and his or her family. The process would be the same as above.

Step Two:
Break Cycles of Abuse

In this Step, you will be asking the Lord to reveal the family sins and iniquities that have been passed on to you from previous generations. First, however, realize that most Christian families are just doing the very best they can, and that it would be wrong to see only their sins and iniquities. Take the time to share with your spouse your answer to the following question:

What habits, customs, traditions and values have you observed in your spouse's family that you really appreciate?

Because of one man (Adam), sin entered into the world and, consequently, all have sinned. This transmission of sin has affected every generation and every people group of the world. The fact that generational cycles of abuse exist is a well-attested social phenomena. This is an opportunity to find freedom in Christ by breaking the stronghold of ancestral sins by making a concerted effort to stop the cycles of abuse.

If we do not face these issues, we will teach what we have been taught, discipline our children the way we have been disciplined and relate to our spouses the way our parents related to each other. Scripture teaches that those who are fully trained will be like their teachers. Childhood training isn't just based on what has been said; it is also based on what has been modeled. Family values are more caught than taught.

When we were born physically alive but spiritually dead, we had neither the presence of God in our life nor the knowledge of His ways. We learned to live our life independently from God. During those formative years, we learned how to cope, survive and succeed without God. When we came to Christ, nobody pushed the "clear" button in our mind. That is why Paul said we must no longer be conformed to this world but be transformed by the renewing of our minds (see Rom. 12:2).

We have all developed many defense mechanisms to protect ourselves. Denial, projection, blaming and many other self-protective behaviors are no longer necessary now that we are new creations in Christ. We are accepted for who we are, and that gives us the freedom to be real and honest. Jesus is our defense. Knowing that we are already forgiven, we can walk in the light and speak the truth in love without fear of rejection.

We can't fix our pasts, but we can be free from them by the grace of God. Trying not to be like our parents or other role models in our lives is still letting those people determine who we are and what we are doing. Strongholds have primarily been erected in our minds from the environments in which we were raised and the traumatic experiences in our pasts. Those strongholds affect our temperaments and the way we relate to our spouses and children. They result in behavior patterns we have learned over time. They will remain unless we renew our minds according to the Word of God.

Start this Step by asking the Lord to mentally reveal the iniquities and family sins your ancestors have passed on to you spiritually and environmentally.

Pray together the following prayer:

Dear heavenly Father,

You are the only perfect parent that we have. We thank You for our natural parents who brought us into this world. We acknowledge they were not perfect, nor were our families and communities in which we grew up. We ask that You reveal to our minds the dysfunctional patterns and family sins of our ancestors that have been going on for generations. Reveal to us the strongholds in our minds that have kept us from fully honoring You and embracing the truth. Give us the grace to face the truth and not to be defensive. Only You can meet our deepest needs of acceptance, security, significance and sense of belonging. We thank You that You have made us new creations in Christ. We desire to be free from our pasts so that we can be all You want us to be.

In Jesus' name, we pray. Amen.

Allow the Lord to reveal any and all family sins of your ancestors. You and your spouse should each consider first your own upbringing and family heritage. Individually and honestly address the following issues, and then write your answers down on a separate paper:

1. What sins seem to be repeated again and again in your family? Lying, criticizing, drinking, compulsive gambling, cheating, pride, bitterness, adultery, divorce?

2. How did your family deal with conflict? How do you now deal with it?

3. How did each member of your family communicate? Can you speak the truth in love?

4. How did your parents discipline their children? How do you?

5. Where did your parents get their significance? Security? Acceptance? Where do you?

6. Did your parents exhibit the spiritual fruit of self control, or were they controllers or enablers? Which are you?

7. What was their religious preference? What non-Christian beliefs (cultic or occultic) or idols did they embrace? (An "idol" can be anything that has greater prominence in their lives than Christ does.)

8. What lies did they believe and live? How has this affected you?

9. What other ancestral sins has God revealed to your mind?

After making your individual lists, share with each other what you have learned. Remember, "there is now no condemnation for those who are in Christ Jesus" (Rom. 8:1) and that we are to accept one another as Christ has accepted us (see 15:7). Mutual sharing allows you to both understand and accept each other.

We are not responsible for our parents' sins, but because our parents sinned we have been taught, trained and disciplined in ways that may not be healthy. Denial and cover-up will only perpetuate the sins of our ancestors and the effects it has on us and on our children. It is our responsibility to face these issues and stop the cycle of abuse so that it is not passed on to the next generation. The Lord instructs us to confess our iniquity and the iniquity of our forefathers (see Lev. 26:40).

Both spouses should now pray the following prayer individually and out loud in each other's presence for every family sin of their ancestors.

Dear heavenly Father,

I confess [name every sin] as sinful and displeasing to You. I turn from it, reject it and ask You to break its hold on me and on our marriage. In Jesus' name. Amen.

We are to confess not only the family sins of our ancestors but also our own sins. Individual and personal sins are dealt with in the personal Steps to Freedom in Christ. However, marriages also have corporate sins that must be confessed and forsaken. Corporate sins are patterns of behavior in marriage that are displeasing to God and contrary to His revealed will. They do not differ from individual sins in nature. Sin is still sin, whether practiced by an individual or by a married couple. A pattern of sinfulness within a marriage, however, calls for husband and wife to deal with it together. Examples of corporate sins within marriage might be:

- Engaging in sinful activities together that displease God and/or offend others.
- Taking part together in non-Christian religious rituals or any cult or occult ceremonies or practices.
- Agreeing together on any sin: covering up for lying, theft, adultery, divorce, cheating on taxes, drunkenness, child abuse, and so on.
- Withholding tithes and offerings from God.
- Falling into patterns of gossip, slander, filthy language or other sins of the tongue in *conversations with each other.*
- Tolerating sinful behavior on the part of your children, especially while they live under your roof, such as swearing, foul language, sex outside of marriage, gambling, alcohol, drugs or anything else that contradicts God's written Word.
- Reading or viewing pornographic material or anything pro-

duced by psychics, mediums, occult practitioners, cults or false religions.

Pray together the following prayer:

Dear heavenly Father,

As we seek You, bring to our minds all the corporate sins that we have committed in our marriage and family. Remind us of the sins of our ancestors and their families. Open our eyes to any tendency to repeat the same dysfunctional patterns. Give us discernment to identify and renounce the corporate sins in our marriage we have tolerated or have not dealt with adequately. Grant us grace that we may confess them, renounce them, turn away from them and commit ourselves never to return to them.

In Jesus' cleansing name, we pray. Amen.

Begin to identify the corporate sins in your marriage. Usually, this Step starts slowly but gradually gains momentum. Be patient and work for general agreement. Write down only those items that you both agree are corporate marriage sins.

In each other's presence, confess all the Lord has revealed to you. Each of you should then ask your spouse's forgiveness for the ways your involvement in these sins has hurt the other and damaged your marriage.

When you both are finished, make the following declaration:

We confess and renounce our own corporate sins and all those sins of our ancestors. We declare by the grace of God that we are new creations in Christ. We commit ourselves and our marriage to the Lord Jesus Christ. We take our place in Christ, and by His authority we command Satan to flee from us, our marriage and our family. We belong to God, and we are a part of His family and under His protection. We put on the armor

of God and commit ourselves to stand firm in our relationship to our
heavenly Father.

Satan's grip from generational sins and cycles of abuse can be broken instantly. However, it will take time to renew your minds and overcome patterns of the flesh. An experienced pastor or committed
Christian counselor can often help in this process.

We must accept one another and build up one another. Growth in
character will also take time, and we must be patient with each other.
Unconditional love and acceptance frees each of us so that we can
accept ourselves and grow in the grace of the Lord.

Conclude this Step with the following prayer:

Dear heavenly Father,

Thank You for Your unconditional love and acceptance. We give our-
selves and each other to You. Enable us by Your grace to accept each other
as You have accepted us and to be merciful as You have been merciful. Show
us how we can build up one another, encourage one another and forgive
one another. We acknowledge that we have not attained the full stature of
Christ, but we desire to be like You in our marriage and in all we do.

We face up to our own corporate sins as well as the family sins of
our ancestors. We honestly confess our participation in them and agree
this behavior is unacceptable to You. We disown them and repudiate
them. In Jesus' name we break all the influence of their dysfunctional
patterns on us and our marriage. We cancel out all advantages,
schemes and other works of the devil that have been passed from our
ancestors to us and to our marriage. We break any foothold or strong-
hold built from the enemy's influence and give our hearts to You for the
renewing of our minds.

We invite the Holy Spirit to apply the shed blood of the Lord Jesus on
Calvary's cross to our corporate sins and to our ancestral sins. Through

God's grace, by faith, we claim the work of Christ in His death and resurrection as our ransom from sin, release from guilt and removal of shame.
In Jesus' precious name, we pray. Amen.

Step Three:
Balance Rights and Responsibilities

In this Step, you will be asking the Lord to reveal to your minds any ungodly ways you have related to each other. We are responsible for our own character and the needs of each other. Scripture teaches us to be submissive to one another, love one another, accept one another and respect one another. Pray together the following prayer, asking the Lord to reveal any ways self-centered living and insistence on your own rights have kept you from assuming your responsibilities to love and accept one another.

Pray together out loud:

Dear heavenly Father,
We thank You for Your full and complete love and acceptance. Thank You that the unselfish sacrifice of Christ's death on the cross and His resurrection met our greatest need for forgiveness and life. We ask You to reveal to our minds any ways we have been selfish in our relationship with each other. Show us how we have not loved each other, not accepted each other, not respected each other and have not been submissive to the needs of each other in the fear of God. Show us how we have been angry, jealous, insecure, manipulative or controlling.
In Jesus' name, we pray. Amen.

Sit silently before the Lord and allow Him to reveal every way you have not:

1. Loved your spouse as you should have
2. Accepted your spouse as you should have
3. Respected your spouse as you should have
4. Submitted to your spouse as you should have
5. Appreciated your spouse as you should have
6. Trusted God to bring conviction and self-control in your spouse

When you have finished completing the above, verbally confess what the Lord has shown you and ask your spouse's forgiveness for not being what God has called you to be. Do not overlook the times and ways that you have communicated rejection, disrespect and lack of appreciation.

Now, without attacking the other person's character, share with each other your personal needs that you feel are not being met. It is legitimate to share a need; it is not legitimate to attack another's character. Then share the times and ways your spouse has shown love, respect and acceptance to you.

Conclude this Step with the following prayer of commitment.

Dear heavenly Father,

We have fallen short of Your glory and have not lived up to our responsibilities. We have been selfish and self-centered. Thank You for Your forgiveness. We commit ourselves to an increasing pattern of love, acceptance and respect for each other. We will submit to each other's needs in reverence to Christ. Restore to us our first love.

In Jesus' name, we pray. Amen.

Step Four:
Break Sexual Bondage

Note: Individual freedom from sexual bondage coming from your own past must be achieved before continuing with this Step. You should have already dealt with this in the individual Steps to Freedom in Christ. If not, you will need to pray individually first, asking the Lord to reveal to your mind every sexual use of your body as an instrument of unrighteousness. As God reveals, renounce each use by saying:

Lord, I renounce [name the specific use of your body such as "having intercourse"] with [name the person], and I ask You to break spiritual, sexual and emotional bond with [name].

Don't bypass anything God brings to your mind, including sensual touching of another or sexual fantasies of another person. (Please refer to the individual Steps for the complete process.)

Scripture teaches that we do not have authority over our own bodies, but that our spouses do (see 1 Cor. 7:1-5). We can and should meet one another's sexual needs. However, our spouses cannot resolve our problems of lust; only Christ can break those bondages. (If either you or your spouse have been struggling with sexual bondage, it may be necessary for you to first read *Finding Freedom in a Sex-Obsessed World* [Harvest House].)

Pray the following out loud together:

Dear heavenly Father,

We know You desire for us to be free from sexual bondage and to be responsive and respectful of each other's needs. Free us from our lust, and may our sexual union be one of honest love and respect for each other. We now ask You to reveal to our minds any way we have sexually violated our marital commitment to each other. Give us the grace to speak the truth in love and the desire to be intimately bonded together sexually. If we have not been honest about our sexual needs and desires, show us how. Give us the freedom to communicate in such a way that our love for each other can be fully expressed.

In Jesus' precious name, we pray. Amen.

Sit silently before the Lord and allow Him to guide you. Ask Him to cover the next few minutes with grace. Sex is a very intimate expression of love and can be a tremendous cause for guilt and insecurity when experienced outside the will of God.

1. In what way have you been dishonest about your sexual relationship together?
2. What have you been doing together that you now believe to be wrong?
3. How have your consciences been violated, or have either of you violated the conscience of the other?

You and you spouse need to answer these questions honestly and seek forgiveness from each other. The best way to find out if you have violated the other person's conscience is to ask!

After you have done this, complete this Step with the following prayer:

Dear heavenly Father,

We stand naked before You. You know the thoughts and intentions of our hearts. We desire to be sexually free before You and with each other. We acknowledge that we have sinned. Thank You for Your forgiveness and cleansing. We now give our bodies to You and to each other as living sacrifices. Fill us with Your Holy Spirit and bond us together in love. May our sexual relationship be holy in Your sight, and may it be an expression of our love for each other.

In Jesus' name, we pray. Amen.

Now declare:

In the name and authority of the Lord Jesus Christ, we command Satan to leave our presence. We present our bodies to the Lord Jesus Christ and reserve the sexual use of our bodies for each other only. We renounce the lie of Satan that sex is dirty or that our bodies are dirty. We stand naked and unashamed before God and each other.

Step Five:
Release Old Hurts

Forgiveness sets us free from our past. It is routinely necessary in any marriage because we don't live with perfect people. Resentment and bitterness will tear us apart. Forgiveness is the first step in reconciliation, which is essential for bonding together. We also need to forgive others so that Satan cannot take advantage of us (see 2 Cor. 2:10-11). We are to be merciful just as our heavenly Father is merciful (see Luke 6:36). We are to forgive as we have been forgiven (see Eph. 4:31-32).

Start this Step by making a timeline, beginning with the day you first met and ending with today, as shown below. Above the line, list all the good memories that you have had together in your marriage. Below the line, list all the painful memories.

Good Memories
First Met ——————————————————————————Today

Thank the Lord, out loud in the presence of each other, for the good memories that have been especially meaningful in your relationship.

Lord, I thank You for [name the good memory].

Painful Memories
After thanking the Lord aloud for the good memories of your marriage, pray together the following prayer. Then follow with a few moments of silent prayer, allowing the Lord to help you recall the painful experiences and traumatic events of your marriage.

Dear heavenly Father,

Sometimes pain has come to us through circumstances, sometimes from other people, sometimes from each other. Whatever the cause, surface in our minds all the pain that You want us to deal with at this time. Let us get in touch with the emotional core of hurt and heartache, trauma and threats that have damaged our marriage. Show us where we have allowed a root of bitterness to spring up, causing trouble and defiling many [see Heb. 12:15].

In Jesus' precious name, we pray. Amen.

Caution! *This step is not a time for casting blame but for sharing pain.* Individually, make lists of painful memories the Lord brings to your minds. Use real names, places and dates as much as possible. It is nearly impossible to get in touch with the emotional core of pain without using people's names and recalling specific events. We easily pick up each other's offenses. We also easily turn bitter toward those we perceive have wrongly influenced our spouses (even when our spouses don't see it). Jealousy can also create bitterness.

One more word of caution: Everything is to be spoken in love and respect. This is not a time for malicious talk. It is a time to bring healing to damaged emotions and to free yourself from your past. Simply record what happened and how you felt about it. You and your spouse can say "amen" when finished. Understand that forgiveness is not forgetting. Forgiveness may lead to forgetting, but trying to forget only complicates forgiveness.

Before you start the forgiveness process, recall these 10 steps to forgiveness:

1. Allow yourself and your spouse to feel the pain, hurt, resentment, bitterness and hate (see Matt. 5:4).
2. Submit to God, recalling how Christ forgave you (see Matt. 18:21-35; Eph. 4:32; Col. 3:13; Jas. 4:7-8).
3. Ask for Christ's grace and power to forgive (see Luke 11:9-10).

4. Agree to live with the unavoidable consequences of the other person's sin against you (see Eph. 5:21).
5. Release the offense. Tear up the moral, personal or relational debt the other person owes you (see Matt. 6:12).
6. Never bring it up again as a weapon against them (see Rom. 12:17).
7. Keep forgiving when your emotions recycle the pain or when the other person keeps offending you (see Matt. 18:21-22).
8. Reject the sinful act and tolerate it no longer (see Rom. 12:21).
9. Turn the vengeance over to God and over to God's human authorities (see Rom. 12:19-20; 13:1).
10. Replace the old resentful feelings with the forgiving love of Christ (see Eph. 4:31-32).

Do not make forgiveness more difficult than it already is. Some things we do *not* have to do include:

- We don't have to feel good about the person who hurt us either before or after we forgive.
- We don't have to tell other people about our resentful feelings unless the Holy Spirit guides us to do so. Matthew 5:23-26 does tell us to seek forgiveness and be reconciled to those we have offended, as the Holy Spirit guides.
- We don't have to wait until we are ready to forgive. We can obey God's Word right now.

Both you and your spouse should bring the painful memories before the Lord, asking for courage to face the pain honestly and for the grace to forgive fully. Releasing the offenses results in relieving the pain. Item by item, individually forgive each person you recall and release the offenses as follows:

Lord, I forgive [name] for [specifically identify all offenses and painful memories].

Prayerfully focus on each person until every remembered pain has surfaced. Be sure to include your husband or wife and every painful memory in your marriage. Both of you should also ask the Lord's forgiveness and forgive yourselves as needed. Bitterness hardens the heart, but forgiveness softens it. After you have completed the above, pray the following prayer, and make the following declaration together out loud:

Dear heavenly Father,

We thank You for Your unconditional love and forgiveness. It is Your kindness and patience that have led us to forgiveness. In the name of Jesus and with His kindness and tenderness, we forgive every person who has ever hurt us, our family or our marriage. We forgive each other for the pain that has come through weakness, poor judgment and outright sin. We accept Your forgiveness of ourselves for the pain and damage caused in our marriage.

By Your grace, bring healing, help and hope to those who have hurt us and to those who have been hurt by us. We bless them all in the name of our Lord Jesus Christ, who taught us, "Love your enemies, do good to those who hate you, bless those who curse you, pray for those who mistreat you" [Luke 6:27-28]. According to Your Word, we pray for those who have hurt us.

In the precious name of Jesus, we pray. Amen.

Together, make the following declaration:

By the authority of the Lord Jesus Christ, who is seated at the heavenly Father's right hand, we assume our responsibility to resist the devil. We declare that we are crucified, buried, made alive, raised up and seated with Christ at the right hand of God. In union with Christ and with His authority, we command Satan to release any foothold on our lives or any influence on our marriage. In the all-powerful name of the cruci-fied, risen and reigning Lord Jesus Christ, we command Satan and all his evil spirits to leave our presence and our marriage. Do not come back. Take away with you all of your lingering effects on our memories, our relationships, our present thoughts and our future together.

Step Six:
Unmask Satan's Deceptions

The goal of Satan is to discredit the work of Christ and tear apart mar-riages and families. His primary weapons are deception, temptation and accusation. He also uses harassment, discouragement and disillusion-ment. The tongue is the instrument the devil uses most. We either become tongue-tied and refuse to speak the truth in love or allow the tongue to become a destructive weapon. When we buy into Satan's lies, we turn against God and each other. Our homes become a battleground instead of a proving ground. Our desire should be for every member of our fami-ly to be a part of the building crew rather than the wrecking crew.

If only one member of the family pays attention to the Holy Spirit, it will have strengthening effects on every other member. On the other hand, if only one member of the family pays attention to a deceiving spir-it, it will have weakening effects on every other member. The purpose of this Step is to unmask the evil one's deceptions and stand in the power of the Holy Spirit against his attacks.

Satan uses real people to mount his attacks. They may be coming from deceived or evil people inside or outside the family (for example, a friend or coworker may lead your spouse into an adulterous affair). The attacks may come through relatives or neighbors who use their tongues as a destructive weapon. They may come from people who give you bad counsel to leave your marriage or abandon your children. They may even possibly come through Satanists who use occultic rituals or blood sacrifices in an evil attempt to destroy families and, therefore, people's testimonies. Ask the Lord to show you the nature of these attacks so that you can stand against them and be united as one family under the lordship of Christ.

Pray the following prayer:

Dear heavenly Father,

We stand under Your authority. We give thanks that You are our hiding place, our protection and our refuge. We clothe ourselves and our marriage with the Lord Jesus Christ and with the full armor of God. We choose to be strong in You, Lord, and in the strength of Your might. We stand firm in our faith, submit to You and resist the devil.

Open our eyes to see the attacks of the evil one against us, our marriage and our family. Give us spiritual discernment to become aware of Satan's schemes, not ignorant of them. Open our eyes to the reality of the spiritual world in which we live. We ask You for the ability to discern spiritually so that we can judge rightly between good and evil.

As we wait silently before You, reveal to us the attacks of Satan against us, our marriage, our family and our ministries so that we may stand against them and expose the father of lies.

In Jesus' discerning name, we pray. Amen.

Make a list of whatever God brings to your mind that may be due to:

- Repetitive thoughts that cause you to close your spirit toward God and each other (see 1 Tim. 4:1; 2 Cor. 10:3-5).
- Recurring times and situations that cause distractions, confusion and disorder in your marriage and in your home—usually during family discussions, devotions and times surrounding church and ministry (see 1 Thess. 2:18).

· Improper stewardship (see 1 Cor. 4:1-2), such as (1) sins that have been tolerated in the home, and (2) anti-Christian material brought into the home.

Sinful activities need to be renounced. Attacks from the enemy due to your obedience to God need to be understood so that you can recognize them and stand against them in the future. As a family, you need to understand that you wrestle not against flesh and blood but against the powers of darkness (see Eph. 6:12). You and your family don't want to be blindfolded warriors who strike out at each other.

When you tear down an established satanic stronghold in your family, you may face some resistance. To walk free from past influences and present attacks, verbally make the following declaration:

As children of God who have been delivered from the power of darkness and translated into the kingdom of God's dear Son, we submit to God and resist the devil. We cancel out all demonic working passed on to us from our ancestors. We have been crucified and raised with our Lord Jesus Christ, and we now sit enthroned with Him in heavenly places.

We renounce all satanic assignments directed toward us, our marriage, our family and our ministry. We cancel every curse Satan and his deceived, misguided or evil workers have put on us and our marriage. We announce to Satan and all his forces that Christ became a curse for us when He died on the cross. We reject any and every way in which Satan may claim ownership of us.

We belong to the Lord Jesus Christ, who purchased us with His own blood. We reject all other occultic rituals and blood sacrifices whereby Satan may claim ownership of us, our marriage and our children. We declare ourselves to be eternally and completely signed over and committed to the Lord Jesus Christ. By the authority we have in Jesus Christ, we now command every familiar spirit and every enemy of the Lord

Jesus Christ to leave our presence and our home forever. We commit ourselves to our heavenly Father to do His will from this day forward.

Now pray the following prayer together:

Dear heavenly Father,

We come to You as Your children, purchased by the blood of the Lord Jesus Christ. You are the Lord of the universe and the Lord of our lives. We yield our rights to You as the Lord of our marriage. We submit our bodies to You as instruments of righteousness, a living sacrifice, that we may glorify You in our bodies and in our marriage. We reserve the sexual use of our bodies for each other only. We now ask You to fill us with Your Holy Spirit. We commit ourselves to the renewing of our minds to prove that Your will is good, perfect and acceptable for us. We commit ourselves to take every thought captive to the obedience of Christ.

All this we do in the name and authority of the Lord Jesus Christ. Amen.

Next, commit your home to the Lord. Have you brought any foreign objects into your home that could serve as an idol or that were once used for a non-Christian religious purpose? These could provide grounds for Satan to have access to your home. Are there any pornographic videos, magazines or books? Occult or false-religion materials? Anything else that needs to be cleansed from your home? Ask the Lord to reveal any such sins or articles in your home. Make a covenant before the Lord to remove all these items from your home, and then burn or destroy them. Now commit your home to the Lord as follows:

Dear heavenly Father,

We acknowledge that You are the Lord of all. All things You have created are good, and You have charged us to be good stewards of all You have entrusted to us. Thank You for all You have provided for our family.

We claim no ownership of what You have entrusted to us. We dedicate our home to You, our living quarters, and our work space and all the property, possessions and finances You have entrusted to us. We promise to remove from our home anything and everything displeasing to You.

We renounce any attacks, devices or ceremonies of the enemy or his people designed to claim any ownership of that with which we have been entrusted. We have been bought and purchased by the blood sacrifice of our Lord Jesus Christ. We claim our home for our family as a place of spiritual safety and protection from the evil one. We renounce anything and everything that has taken place in our home by us, or by those who have lived in our house before us, that does not please You, our heavenly Father. We ask for Your divine protection around our home and our family. We desire to honor You in all our ways. Thank You for Your protection.

Dear Lord, You are the King of our lives and our marriage, and we exalt You. May all that we do bring honor and glory to You.

In Jesus' holy name, we pray. Amen.

Then declare:

As children of God, seated with Christ in the heavenly places, we command every evil spirit to leave our presence and our home. We renounce all curses and spells against our house, property, possessions and our very selves. We announce to Satan and all his workers that our marriage, our family and all that our heavenly Father has entrusted to us belong to the Lord Jesus Christ. We submit them all to the direction and control of the Holy Spirit.

Step Seven:
Renew Christian Marriage

All who marry, whether Christian or not, become part of God's creation order of marriage (see Gen. 1:26-28; 2:18-25). A "creation order" is a God-given longing built into the fabric of human life. As a result of this

God-given longing, every culture and all people groups on Earth practice marriage in some form. Violating marriage breaks the order of creation and always brings terrible consequences.

When one partner (or both) knows Jesus Christ as Lord and Savior, the marriage becomes sanctified or set apart as holy, part of God's new Christian order (see 1 Cor. 7:14). That person commits himself or herself to Christ's new creation in marriage and enters a marriage covenant before God and one another. Christian marriage far exceeds a mere social contract. Marriage as a social contract is only a legal agreement between two parties. Christian marriage is a lifelong covenant with binding vows, spoken before God and human witnesses. If the vows are broken, they bring God's judgment. If they are kept, they bring God's rewards.

Satan's lie is that we are married singles, bound only by a human relationship and a social contract. That means marriage can be broken whenever either party feels the partners have irreconcilable differences. In Christ, there are no irreconcilable differences. We have been reconciled to Him, and we have been given the ministry of reconciliation.

God's truth is that the marriage vows bind us through the organic union of Christian marriage. A new creation lasts until the death of one of the spouses. A contract can be canceled, but a new creation lasts a lifetime. Contracts can be broken or renegotiated, but a new creation either grows toward fulfillment or is violated.

Living in obedience to God's Word in Christian marriage (or any other part of life) brings the Lord's shelter of protection (see Ps. 91). It results in God's blessings, including children who are set apart for God's purposes (see 1 Cor. 7:14). By God's grace, His blessings extend not only to those who are faithful to Him but also to their descendants for many generations to come (see Exod. 20:6; Deut. 7:9; Luke 1:50). Violating a marriage covenant brings God's curse, not only on ourselves, but also on our descendants for three or four more generations (see Exod. 20:5; 34:7; Num. 14:18; Jer. 32:18).

Verbally make the following declaration by speaking the words aloud and in unison:

Satan, we renounce you in all your works and all your ways. We submit ourselves and our marriage to God, and we resist the devil. In the all-powerful name of the Lord Jesus Christ, we command you to leave our marriage. Take all of your deceitful spirits, evil demons and fallen angels with you, and go to the place where the Lord Jesus Christ sends you. Leave us and our marriage, and don't come back. Take with you all of your temptations to violate our marriage vows. Take with you all of your accusing and demeaning thoughts we could think against each other. Take with you all of your deceptions that contradict God's written Word. The Lord Jesus Christ has torn down your demonic authority, and we stand against your influence and activity toward our lives and our marriage.

You are a defeated foe, disarmed of your weapons, and were made a public spectacle by the cross of Christ [see Col. 2:15]. Greater is He who is in us than he who is in the world [see 1 John 4:4]. The prince of this world now stands condemned [see John 16:11]. Christ has the supremacy over every evil throne, power, rule or authority [see Col. 1:16]. Jesus shared our humanity that by His death He might destroy him who holds the power of death, that is, the devil [see Heb. 2:14]. We resist you by the authority of Christ and because we are alive in Him. Therefore, you must flee from us [see Jas. 4:7].

Now pray aloud together:

Dear heavenly Father,

We gladly acknowledge that You created marriage and family life for Your glory. Thank You for designing marriage as a creation order, woven into the fabric of human society. We commit ourselves anew to a covenant of Christian marriage with all its blessings.

We renounce the devil's lie that we are married singles, bound only by a human relationship and a social contract. We recall that our marriage is binding as long as we both shall live. We acknowledge that we can never violate our marriage vows without bringing lasting damage on ourselves, our children and our descendants for three or four generations to come.

We confess we have not perfectly lived up to our marriage vows. We confess we have not always lived as one in Christ. We have fallen short of Your perfect will by our own selfishness and sin. We gladly accept Your forgiveness of our sins through the blood of Christ on the cross [see 1 John 2:1-2]. By grace through faith, we receive Christ's abundant life into our hearts and His holiness into our marriage [see John 10:10; 1 Cor. 7:1]).

We crucify our own fleshly lusts and sinful desires that tempt us to ignore or violate our marriage vows [see 1 Pet. 2:11; Gal. 5:24]. We clothe ourselves and our marriage with the Lord Jesus Christ and His armor of light [see Rom. 13:12-14; Gal. 3:26-27]. We give ourselves to live by the Spirit in daily obedience to Christ [see Gal. 5:16; 1 Pet. 1:2].

We announce that in Christ we have all the spiritual blessings we need to live out our new creation. We affirm that we are one in Christ Jesus— one marriage, one flesh, one family [see Eph. 1:3; 3:14-15; Gen. 2:24; Mark 10:6-9]. We submit ourselves and our marriage to the ownership of our heavenly Father, to the lordship of Jesus Christ and to the power of the Holy Spirit. From this day forward, we ask You to use our marriage to display Your splendor before our children. We invite You to work through us to show Your glory in the midst of a corrupt and wicked generation.

In Jesus' glorious name. Amen.

When you and your spouse were first married, you spoke vows that said, "I take you as my lawful wedded wife or husband." In the following renewal of vows, you will become a giver instead of a taker. Please note the slight change in wording in this vow from I *take you* as my wedded husband or wife to I *give myself to you* to be your husband or wife.

As you hold hands and face each other, first the husband, and then the wife, should repeat the following. (In a group setting, a minister of the gospel can lead this renewal of marriage vows.)

I [name] give myself to you, [name], to be your wedded [husband or wife], to have and to hold from this day forward, for better or for worse, for richer or for poorer, in sickness and in health, to love and to cherish, until death do us part, according to God's holy Word; and hereto, I pledge you my faithfulness.

Living Free in Christ

Freedom must be maintained. You have won a very important battle in an ongoing war. You will continue to experience your freedom as long as you keep choosing truth and standing firm in the strength of the Lord. If more painful memories should surface, or if you become aware of lies you have been living, renounce them and choose the truth. (Some couples have found it helpful to go through these steps again.)

If you haven't already done so, please read *Victory Over the Darkness* and *The Bondage Breaker*. We also suggest that you read Neil's book *Discerning God's Will in Spiritually Deceptive Times* (Harvest House), which was written to help people understand God's guidance so that they can discern counterfeit guidance. To maintain your freedom, we also suggest the following:

- Become active together in a Christ-centered church. Build healthy allies for your marriage.

- Study your Bible daily, pray and be sensitive to the leading of the Holy Spirit. We also suggest reading one chapter together every day of *Who I Am in Christ* (Regal Books) for the next 36 days. Then use the devotional *Daily in Christ* (Harvest House) by Neil and Joanne Anderson or *The Daily Discipler* (Regal Books) by Neil.

- Review and apply your personal freedom in Christ. Remind yourselves of your identity in Christ, winning the battle for the mind and processing the Steps to Freedom in Christ (personal freedom) as an ongoing personal inventory. The Lord uses marriage to reveal the layers of our selfishness and immaturity, which He wants to peel off.

- Take every thought captive to the obedience of Christ. Assume responsibility for private thoughts, reject the lies, choose the truth and stand firm in your identity in Christ.

- Don't drift away! It is very easy to get lazy in your thoughts and revert back to old habit patterns of thinking. Share struggles openly with each other.

- Don't expect your spouse to fight your battles. Although you can help each other, no one else can think, pray or read the Bible for you.

- If serious problems still persist, seek out a competent Christian pastor or counselor who is committed to the biblical institution of marriage.

Pray with confidence as follows:

Dear heavenly Father,

We honor You as our sovereign Lord. We acknowledge that You are always present with us. You are the only all-powerful and all-knowing God.

You are kind and loving in all Your ways. We love You. We thank You that we are united together with Christ, and we are spiritually alive in Him. We choose not to love the world, and we crucify the flesh and all its sinful desires.

We thank You that we are children of God, new creations in Christ Jesus and filled with His eternal life. We ask You to fill us with Your Holy Spirit so that we may live our lives free from sin. We declare our dependence on You, and we take our stand against Satan and all his lying ways. We choose to believe the truth, and we refuse to be discouraged or to give up hope for our marriage. You are the God of all hope, and we are confident that You will meet our needs as we seek to live according to Your Word. We express with confidence that we can live a responsible life and be faithful in our marriage through Christ who strengthens us.

We ask these things in the precious name of our Lord and Savior, Jesus Christ. Amen.

Make the following declaration together:

We now take our stand in Christ and we put on the whole armor of God. In union with Christ, we command Satan and all his evil spirits to depart from us. We submit our bodies to God as living sacrifices and renew our minds by the living Word of God so that we may prove the will of God is good, acceptable and perfect.

Now read the declarations from the "We Are One in Christ" chart on the following page out loud together:

We Are One in Christ

We Are Accepted in Christ:

John 1:12	We are God's children.
John 15:15	We are Christ's friends.
Romans 5:1	We have been justified.
1 Corinthians 6:17	We are united with the Lord and one with Him in spirit.
1 Corinthians 6:20	We have been bought with a price; we belong to God.
1 Corinthians 12:27	We are members of Christ's Body.
Ephesians 1:1	We are saints.
Ephesians 1:5	We have been adopted as God's children.
Ephesians 2:18	We have direct access to God through the Holy Spirit.
Colossians 1:14	We have been redeemed and forgiven of all our sins .
Colossians 2:10	We are complete in Christ.

We Are Secure in Christ:

Romans 8:1-2	We are free from condemnation.
Romans 8:28	We are assured that all things work together for good.
Romans 8:33-34	We are free from any condemning charges against us.
Romans 8:35	We cannot be separated from the love of God.
2 Corinthians 1:21	We have been established, anointed and sealed by God.
Colossians 3:3	We are hidden with Christ in God.
Philippians 1:6	We are confident that the good work God has begun in us will be perfected.
Philippians 3:20	We are citizens of heaven.
2 Timothy 1:7	We have not been given a spirit of fear, but of power, love and a sound mind.
Hebrews 4:16	We can find grace and mercy in time of need.
1 John 5:18	We are born of God and the evil one cannot touch us.

We Are Significant in Christ:

Matthew 5:13-14	We are the salt and light of the earth.
John 15:1,5	We are a branch of the true vine, a channel of His life.
John 15:16	We have been chosen and appointed to bear fruit.
Acts 1:8	We are personal witnesses of Christ's.
1 Corinthians 3:16	We are God's temple.
2 Corinthians 5:17-20	We are ministers of reconciliation.
2 Corinthians 6:1	We are God's coworkers .
Ephesians 2:6	We are seated with Christ in the heavenly realm.
Ephesians 2:10	We are God's workmanship.
Ephesians 3:12	We may approach God with freedom and confidence.
Philippians 4:13	We can do all things through Christ who strengthens us.

MATERIALS AND TRAINING FOR YOU AND YOUR CHURCH

There have been several exploratory studies that have shown promising results regarding the effectiveness of the Steps to Freedom in Christ. Judith King, a Christian Therapist, did several pilot studies in 1996. All three of these studies were conducted on participants who attended a Living Free in Christ conference and processed the Steps to Freedom in Christ during the conference.

The first study involved 30 participants who took a 10-item questionnaire before completing the Steps. The questionnaire was re-administered 3 months after their participation. The questionnaire assessed for levels of depression, anxiety, inner conflict, tormenting thoughts and addictive behaviors.

The second study involved 55 participants who took a 12-item questionnaire before completing the Steps and then re-administered 3 months later.

The third study involved 21 participants who also took a 12-item questionnaire before receiving the Steps and then again 3 months later.

The following table illustrates the percentage of improvement for each category.

	Depression	Anxiety	Inner Conflict	Tormenting Thoughts	Addictive Behavior
Pilot Study 1	64%	58%	63%	82%	52%
Pilot Study 2	47%	44%	51%	58%	43%
Pilot Study 3	52%	47%	48%	57%	39%

Research was also conducted by doctoral students at Regent University under the supervision of Dr. Fernando Garzon, Doctor of Psychology, on the message and method of Discipleship Counseling Ministries.

Most people attending a Living Free in Christ conference can work through the repentance process on their own using the Steps to Freedom in Christ. As we mentioned in the Introduction, in our experience, about 15 percent can't because of difficulties they have experienced. For these individuals, we offered a personal session with a trained encourager. They were given a pretest before a Step session and a posttest three months later. The following were the results, as given in terms of percentage of improvement:

	Oklahoma City, OK	Tyler, TX
Depression	44%	57%
Anxiety	45%	54%
Fear	48%	49%
Anger	36%	55%
Tormenting Thoughts	51%	50%
Negative Habits	48%	53%
Sense of Self-worth	52%	56%

The materials for training encouragers include books, study guides and cassette series (both video and audio), and DVD series. The audio-cassettes have corresponding syllabi. The training is best facilitated if the trainees watch the videos or DVDs, read the books and complete the study guides. The study guides will greatly increase the learning process and help people to personalize and internalize the message. Should the cost prohibit some from using the videos, the books and study guides can still be effective. We recommend a 16-week training period that meets 2 hours per week with the following schedule:

First Four Weeks

Video/DVD/Audio Series: "Resolving Personal Conflicts"

Reading: *Victory Over the Darkness* and study guide

Second Four Weeks

Video/ DVD/Audio Series: "Resolving Spiritual Conflicts"

Reading: *The Bondage Breaker* and study guide

Third and Fourth Four Weeks

Video/ DVD/Audio Series: "Discipleship Counseling" and "How to Lead a Person to Freedom in Christ"

Reading: *Discipleship Counseling* and *Released from Bondage*

Suppose your church carefully chose 20 people and trained them as outlined above. If each person agreed to help just one other person every other week, by the end of one year, your church would have helped 520 people. The ministry wouldn't stop there, for these people would become witnesses without even trying. Your church would become known in the community as a ministry that really cares for people—and one that has an answer for the problems of life. What kind of a witness do Christians have if they are living in bondage? Children of God who are established alive and free in Christ will naturally (supernaturally) be witnesses as they glorify God by bearing fruit.

Books and Resources by
Dr. Neil T. Anderson

About Dr. Neil T. Anderson

Dr. Neil T. Anderson was formerly the chairman of the Practical Theology Department at Talbot School of Theology. In 1989, he founded Freedom in Christ Ministries, which now has staff and offices in various countries around the world. In 2001, Dr. Anderson stepped down as president of Freedom in Christ Ministries and officially retired in May 2005 in order to start Discipleship Counseling Ministries. The purpose of this new ministry is to give greater focus to his personal speaking and writing ministry and to allow him more flexibility to serve others without financial constraints. For more information about Dr. Anderson and his ministry, visit his website at www.discipleshipcounselingministries.org.

Core Message and Materials

Victory Over the Darkness with study guide, audiobook and DVD (Regal Books, 2000). With over 1,000,000 copies in print, this core book explains who you are in Christ, how to walk by faith in the power of the Holy Spirit, how to be transformed by the renewing of your mind, how to experience emotional freedom, and how to relate to one another in Christ.

The Bondage Breaker with study guide, audiobook (Harvest House Publishers, 2000) and DVD (Regal Books, 2006). With over 1,000,000 copies in print, this book explains spiritual warfare, what our protection is, ways that we are vulnerable, and how we can live a liberated life in Christ.

Discipleship Counseling with DVD (Regal Books, 2003). This book combines the concepts of discipleship and counseling and teaches the practical integration of theology and psychology for helping Christians resolve their personal and spiritual conflicts through repentance and faith in God.

Steps to Freedom in Christ and interactive videocassette (Regal Books, 2004). This discipleship counseling tool helps Christians resolve their personal and spiritual conflicts.

Helping Others Find Freedom in Christ DVD (Regal Books, 2007). In this DVD package, Neil explains the seven Steps to Freedom and how to apply them through discipleship counceling. It gives a thorough explanation of the biblical basis for the steps and helps viewers understand the root cause of personal and spiritual problems.

Beta: The Next Step in Your Journey with Christ (Regal Books, 2004) is a discipleship course for Sunday School classes and small groups. The kit includes a teacher's guide, a student guide and two DVDs covering 12 lessons and the Steps to Freedom in Christ. This course is designed to enable new and stagnant believers to resolve personal and spiritual conflicts and be established alive and free in Christ.

The Daily Discipler (Regal Books, 2005). This practical systematic theology is a culmination of all of Neil's books covering the major doctrines of the Christian faith and the problems they face. It is a five-day-per-week, one-year study that will thoroughly ground believers in their faith.

Victory Over the Darkness Series

Overcoming a Negative Self-Image, with Dave Park (Regal, 2003)
Overcoming Addictive Behavior, with Mike Quarles (Regal, 2003)
Overcoming Doubt (Regal, 2004)
Overcoming Depression, with Joanne Anderson (Regal, 2004) and DVD (2007)

Bondage Breaker Series

Praying by the Power of the Spirit (Harvest House Publishers, 2003)
Finding God's Will in Spiritually Deceptive Times (Harvest House Publishers, 2003)
Finding Freedom in a Sex-Obsessed World (Harvest House Publishers, 2004)

Specialized Books

God's Power at Work in You, with Dr. Robert Saucy (Harvest House Publishers, 2001). A thorough analysis of sanctification and practical instruction on how we grow in Christ.

Released from Bondage, with Judith King and Dr. Fernando Garzon (Thomas Nelson, 2002). This book has personal accounts of defeated Christians with explanatory notes of how they resolved their conflicts and found their freedom in Christ, and how the message of Discipleship Counseling can be applied to therapy with research results.

Daily in Christ, with Joanne Anderson (Harvest House Publishers, 2000). This popular daily devotional is also being used by thousands of Internet subscribers every day.

Who I Am in Christ (Regal Books, 2001). In 36 short chapters, this book describes who you are in Christ and how He meets your deepest needs.

Freedom from Addiction, with Mike and Julia Quarles (Regal Books, 1997). Using Mike's testimony, this book explains the nature of chemical addictions and how to overcome them in Christ.

One Day at a Time, with Mike and Julia Quarles (Regal Books, 2000). This devotional helps those who struggle with addictive behaviors and explains how to discover the grace of God on a daily basis.

Freedom from Fear, with Rich Miller (Harvest House Publishers, 1999). This book explains anxiety disorders and how to overcome them.

Extreme Church Makeover, with Charles Mylander (Regal Books, 2006). This book offers guidelines and encouragement for resolving seemingly impossible corporate conflicts in the church and also provides leaders with a primary means for church growth—releasing the power of God in the church.

Experiencing Christ Together, with Dr. Charles Mylander (Regal Books, 2006.) This book explains God's divine plan for marriage and the steps that couples can take to resolve their difficulties.

Christ Centered Therapy, with Dr. Terry and Julie Zuehlke (Zondervan Publishing House, 2000). A textbook explaining the practical integration of theology and psychology for professional counselors.

Getting Anger Under Control, with Rich Miller (Harvest House Publishers, 1999). This book explains the basis for anger and how to control it.

The Biblical Guide to Alternative Medicine, with Dr. Michael Jacobson (Regal Books, 2003). This book develops a grid by which you can evaluate medical practices, and then applies the grid to the world's most recognized philosophies of medicine and health.

Breaking the Strongholds of Legalism, with Rich Miller and Paul Travis (Harvest House Publishers, 2003). An explanation of legalism and how to overcome it.

Free, with Dave Park (Regal Books, 2005). A 40-day devotional on sanctification.

To purchase the above material, contact the following:
Freedom In Christ Ministries
9051 Executive Park Drive, Suite 503
Knoxville, Tennessee 37923
(866) 462-4747
info@ficm.org

E-3 Resources
317 Main Street, Suite 207
Franklin, Tennessee 37064
(888) 354-9411
info@e3resources.org

For ministry information, visit
www.discipleshipcounselingministries.org

Contact Freedom in Christ Ministries at the following:
Freedom in Christ Ministries
9051 Executive Park Drive, Suite 503
Knoxville, TN 37923
Telephone: (866) 462-4747
E-mail: info@ficm.org
Website: www.ficm.org

For product, contact:
E-3 Resources
317 Main Street
Suite 207
Franklin, Tennessee 327064
(888) 354-9411
info@e3resources.org

Also visit
www.regalbooks.com